Charter versus Federalism:
The Dilemmas of Constitutional Reform

Formal constitutional change is the most demanding and significant political activity available to a free people. According to Alan Cairns, Canadians are very bad at that task; he suggests that an understanding of the lessons of Meech Lake may improve their performance in future.

Cairns's constitutional-sociology approach casts new light on the triumphs and failures of recent decades. Chapter 1 shows how the evolution of the Canadian constitution is profoundly influenced by socio-intellectual forces from outside the country. Chapter 2 explains that the constitution is a powerful instrument to shape Canadians, not just a framework within which individuals pursue private goals.

In chapters 3 and 4, the author analyses the Constitution Act (1982) and Meech Lake (1987–90). As Cairns seeks to establish, the Charter of Rights transformed Canada's constitutional order and challenged the federal principle. It gave expression to non-territorial distinctions that differed from the historical dichotomies of federalism and of the French-English relationship. The amending formula established in 1982 added yet another complexity to the process of constitutional reform, and the Meech Lake process brought into stark relief both the old and the new tensions within Canada's constitution, suggesting lessons that the author distils in chapter 4.

ALAN C. CAIRNS is a professor in the Department of Political Science, University of British Columbia.

Charter versus Federalism

The Dilemmas of Constitutional Reform

ALAN C. CAIRNS

McGill-Queen's University Press
Montreal & Kingston • London • Buffalo

© McGill-Queen's University Press 1992
ISBN 0-7735-0891-0 (cloth)
ISBN 0-7735-0892-9 (paper)

Legal deposit first quarter 1992
Bibliothèque nationale du Québec

Printed in Canada on acid-free paper
Reprinted in paperback 1993

This book has been published
with the help of a grant from the
Social Science Federation of Canada,
using funds provided by the
Social Sciences and Humanities
Research Council of Canada.
Publication has been supported
also by a grant from the
Institute of Intergovernmental Relations,
Queen's University.

Canadian Cataloguing in Publication Data

Cairns, Alan C.
  Charter versus federalism

  Includes bibliographical references.
  ISBN: 978-0-7735-0892-7
  (pbk.)
  1. Civil rights – Canada. 2. Canada – Constitutional
  law – Amendments. I. Title.
  JL31.C327 1992   342.71'085   C91-090604-1

Typeset in Baskerville 10/12 by Caractéra inc.,
Quebec City.

Contents

Foreword

Professor Alan Cairns originally presented the first three of these essays while he was the Kenneth R. MacGregor Visiting Lecturer at Queen's University in February 1987. He revised the text of the lectures and added a fourth essay in order to comment more fully on the developments in constitutional reform which arose after the now famous meeting of Canada's first ministers at Meech Lake in April 1987.

The essays consider the role of the constitution in Canadian society, focusing on how the Charter of Rights and Freedoms introduced in 1982 has transformed the political agenda and the nature of political discourse in Canada. In the process the constitution has become a citizens' rather than a governments' document, central to defining the rights of citizens in the face of international and domestic constraints. Professor Cairns addresses the sociological purposes of the constitution, the importance of competing conceptions of community, and the significance of the 1982 reforms. In the final essay, he analyses the debate over the Meech Lake Accord, which underscored the social role that the constitution now plays.

The MacGregor Lectureship was established to allow the Institute of Intergovernmental Relations to bring to Queen's University each year a distinguished individual who has made an important contribution to the understanding or practice of federalism, intergovernmental relations, or related issues in Canada and other countries. The lectureship honours Kenneth R. MacGregor, a Queen's graduate, longtime member of the University Board of Trustees, former Superintendent of Insurance in Canada, and retired Chairman of the Mutual Life Assurance Company of Canada. The lectureship is funded through the generosity of Mutual Life, members of the Board of Trustees, and friends of Ken MacGregor. Apart from Alan Cairns, the lectureships have been held by Robert Stanfield, Peter Lougheed, Allan Blakeney, Albert Breton, and Gordon Robertson.

Alan Cairns is one of the leading analysts of the Canadian federal system. A graduate of the University of Toronto and Oxford, Professor Cairns has been a member of the faculty of the University of British Columbia since 1960. His insightful comments and critiques of constitutional politics and of the institutions and dynamics of Canadian federalism have been published in many books and articles. He has influenced a generation of Canadian students and shaped in no small measure the way in which Canadians view their constitution.

The Institute of Intergovernmental Relations is pleased to collaborate with McGill-Queen's University Press in the publication of these revised MacGregor Lectures.

Douglas Brown
Acting Director
Institute of Intergovernmental Relations
October 1991

Acknowledgments

Earlier versions of chapters 1–3 were delivered as the MacGregor Lectures at Queen's University in March 1987. Unfortunately, I was unable to revise them for publication immediately. Since the Meech Lake constitutional package to bring Quebec back into the constitutional family, as the prime minister phrased it, was negotiated and made public a few months later, it was impossible to revise these lectures as if the accord had never happened. Consequently, references to Meech Lake are scattered through chapters 1–3 and chapter 4 attempts to extract the major constitutional lessons that can be drawn from the entire affair.

I am grateful to Queen's University and the MacGregor Lectureship for the opportunity to deliver the MacGregor Lectures. The Institute of Intergovernmental Relations was a gracious host in the week my wife, Pat, and I spent at Queen's in March 1987. I owe special thanks to Peter Leslie, then director of the institute, and to his successor, Ronald Watts, director when the finished manuscript was delivered more than three years later. Patience appears to be no less a virtue for those who write about constitutional reform than for those who attempt to bring it about. Supplementary thanks are owed to Ronald Watts, who provided me with helpful suggestions for revision, to some of which I have been able to respond. My continuing medieval dependence on an ancient manual typewriter is possible only because of my complementary reliance on Petula Muller for word-processing assistance; I deeply appreciate her diligence and enthusiastic help. My final thanks are to John Parry, the monograph's copy-editor, who ruthlessly challenged my frequent descent into verbosity.

The three chapters that follow the Introduction are, perhaps, an uneasy mix of the lecture format and the academic article or short monograph. I have tried to preserve the lecture style as appropriate to the context in which the lectures were delivered. That format accounts for the rhetoric and the preachiness that may intrude. It also explains my use of "we" as appropriate to the Canadian audience I was addressing. Every genre has a style appropriate to its nature, which I have tried to respect.[1] Nevertheless, the lapse of months and years has necessitated considerable revision and occasioned an attempt, albeit unsuccessful, to keep on top of the literature that has appeared. The deskbound task of rewriting may have made the manner of expression closer to the written word meant to be read than to the written word meant to be read out to an audience. Such ambiguities, dilemmas, and imperfections are possibly an appropriate self-inflicted punishment for an author whose attempt to shed some light on where we are now in constitutional terms has taken as long to complete as the Meech Lake effort.

Alan C. Cairns

Charter versus Federalism

Introduction

The unity of the following chapters, aside from being contained within the same covers and written by a single author, resides in a particular perspective on the constitution and its relation to Canadian society.[1] The constitution that is portrayed in the following pages, and even more so the Charter, are not the lawyers' constitution and the lawyers' Charter. My interest is more in the social role of the constitution, how it shapes society as it responds to the changing nature of the social and other divisions of a modern people, and the converse, the consequences for the constitution of its tighter embrace of the Canadian people as it detaches itself from its British origins.

The traditional cleavages of federalism that required the constitution to fashion harmonious coexistence between our federal and provincial selves now encompass a diminishing proportion of who we are as a political people. They have been joined by new cleavages or reinvigorated old cleavages related to sex, ethnicity, the aboriginal communities, the disabled, and others. The language of federalism is not central to these newly politicized social categories. Rather, those who speak for them see their "clientele" as possessing some common condition, such as sex or ethnic background, or as experiencing some situation particular to themselves, such as some shared physical or mental disability that has major consequences for the way they live and the treatment they receive from their fellow citizens.

These groups have all developed enhanced constitutional self-consciousness as a result of being drawn into the extended bout of constitutional introspection that Canadians have recently undergone. Further, the constitution now speaks to them through the various clauses that single out specific characteristics as meriting specific Charter recognition. Thus section 27, by specifying that the Charter is to be interpreted "in a manner consistent with the preservation and enhancement of the multicultural heritage of Canadians," speaks to those who are neither aboriginal Canadians nor descendants of the French and English "founding" peoples.[2] Other clauses address the aboriginal peoples (section 25), women (section 28),[3] and official language minorities (section 23), and section 15 singles out various characteristics that "in particular" should not be used to deprive an individual of his/her right to be "equal before and under the law and ... to the equal protection and equal benefit of the law."

These clauses, and the other rights and freedoms of the Charter, give Canadians a direct linkage to the constitution they formerly lacked. The Charter gives constitutional identities and a legitimate basis for making further constitutional claims to those it recognizes in both general and specific terms. They are no longer constitutional outsiders. In a few short years, the Charter has generated a vast, qualitatively impressive discourse organized around rights. This citizen-state discourse is a counter-discourse to the traditional language of federalism to which the constitution gave privileged status prior to 1982. A central task of our constitutional future thus becomes the finding of a rapprochement between a federalism discourse, of special interest to and dominated by governments, and the Charter discourse, which is more democratic in the elementary sense that it involves an extensive cast of citizen actors.

The constitutional conversation precipitated by the Charter is not confined to court rooms and does not require a law degree of its participants. On the contrary, the Charter elevates the significance of citizenship as a dynamic political category in all the arenas in which civic roles can be played. Those who claim rights are not supplicants, and those who respect them are not aristocratic benefactors generously exercising discretion in the expectation of gratitude. As Alexis de Tocqueville wrote: "There is nothing which, generally speaking, elevates and sustains the human spirit more than the idea of rights. There is something great and virile in the idea of right which removes from any request its suppliant character, and places the one who claims it on the same level as the one who grants it."[4] This equalizing aspect of rights makes the Charter a democratizing instrument supportive of a participant political culture.[5]

This democratizing overspill is especially evident in constitutional forums. The various federal and provincial legislative committees dealing with Meech Lake were besieged in English Canada by representatives of various citizen groups which, almost with unanimity, protested the attempt of governments, employing the new 1982 amending formula, to monopolize the amendment process to the end of implementing the Meech Lake agreement. The opponents of

Meech Lake employed remarkably vehement language in their denunciation of what they saw as an illegitimate intergovernmental coup d'état.[6]

Their language suggests that the Charter has taken root and is now part of the civic identity of many Canadians. Its successful grafting onto the Canadian constitutional order is attributable partly to the persuasive effect of various international phenomena, especially the weakening link with the United Kingdom that diminished support for parliamentary supremacy, and an international rights culture given organizational expression by the United Nations.

The international factors behind the Charter are examined in the first chapter. The chapter's larger intellectual purpose is to portray the evolving constitutional order of a modern state as looking outward, as receiving cues and messages from the international environment that redefine what are appropriate contemporary expressions of statehood. As these are assimilated by political élites, opinion leaders, and citizens, they interact with domestic forces to make up the pressures nudging the constitutional order in new directions.

While, on the face of it, this appears to be an unexceptional conclusion, it nevertheless is intended as a salutary reminder to political scientists in particular, myself included, to be less inward-looking as they search for the pressure points confronting the constitutional order. While lawyers are much more sensitive to the interaction of national and international legal norms and instruments, and thus to the international dimension of states' constitutional orders, their writings, at least from a political science perspective, are often insufficiently informed by political and societal considerations. What is needed, and what this first chapter only haltingly provides, is a sociological perspective that identifies the constitution as being one of the crucial meeting points of domestic and international forces. Both of the latter must be broadly defined to include ideas, values, and symbols, which are obviously central to any constitutional order.

The contemporary citizen is subjected to an unceasing flow of international cultural products, values, and ideas that mocks the borders of modern states. The struggle of indigenous peoples, heightened feminist self-consciousness, the politicization of ethnicity, sustained attacks on the theory and practice of racial discrimination, the rights consciousness stimulated by the United Nations, the proliferation of alternative life-styles and family structures and the accompanying demands of gays and lesbians for recognition and respect for their differences – these are all linked to international movements. They all influence our identities, values, and goals. Their consequences for policy extend to the constitution itself, the master policy instrument for the regulation of relations between citizen and state. The limited attempt of the first chapter to apply this perspective to the Charter is tentative and exploratory, rather than comprehensive and reasonably definitive. It clearly needs supplementing. I expect, however, that the latter exercise would refine, not repudiate, the chapter's basic message.

The second chapter, by means of both historical examples and more recent constitutional proposals, discusses the consequences for conceptions of community and citizens' identity of a handful of proposals for constitutional change, some of which never got off the drawing board and others of which were implemented in whole or in part. The chapter's elementary message is that to an indeterminate, but non-trivial extent, the self-conceptions of citizens are derivative of constitutional arrangements. The governing élites of modern states are unlikely to forget that the communities over which they preside require nurturing and that over the long run a Darwinian process sorts out winners and losers, awarding survival to states that succeed in this task and the graveyard to those that do not. Thus in the recent constitutional struggle over the future of Quebec in or out of Canada, and the parallel struggle between (some of) the other provincial governments and the federal government, the stakes were high. "It was for possession of our souls that the contending governments fought,"[7] for their own futures were at stake, and citizens' allegiance was the ultimate political resource. The understanding that community is not a given, but an ever-renewed creation, is unlikely to be forgotten by governing élites and politically aware citizens in heterogeneous polities such as Canada.

Chapter 3 discusses the Constitution Act, 1982, with special reference to the Charter and somewhat less to the amending formula. It concludes that their uneasy coexistence in the same document is unstable, because they disagree on the fundamental purpose of the constitution and for whose benefit it exists. The tension between them derives from the following syllogism:

1 - The Charter gives citizens rights against governments.
2 - The amending formula gives governments a monopoly on formal constitutional change.
3 - Charter rights, accordingly, are conditional on governments not abusing their monopoly of the amending power.

The constitution is seen, therefore, as making simultaneously two contradictory statements about sovereignty, with all the symbolism that that involves. In Pierre Trudeau's oft-repeated phrase, the Charter says that the rights of people precede those of governments. The amending formula states that sovereignty resides in a collective of governments that can amend the constitution in terms of their own self-interest and announce the results as a fait accompli, assuming that legislatures can be kept under control.

In somewhat different language, the Constitution Act, 1982, displays two competing visions of the relation of the constitution to the peoples and governments of Canada. The amending formula presupposes that federalism is the most important constitutional organizing principle, that governments are the major actors in federalism, and that accordingly amendment of the constitution that determines their status and power within federalism is properly a matter for those governments to handle. This "governments' constitution" contrasts with the "citizens' constitution" generated by the Charter, which presupposes that the citizen state axis is no less fundamental than the federal–provincial constitutional axis. Accordingly, citizens via the Charter are just as much part of the constitution as are provincial governments by virtue of section 92 of the Constitution Act, 1867, allocating law-making power to provincial legislatures.

From another perspective, these two views represent older (governments' constitution) and newer (citizens' constitution) orientations that were brought together in the two major components of the Constitution Act, 1982: the amending formula and the Charter. Conceptually, the "governments' constitution," although rooted in the traditional practices of Canadian federalism, especially relating to constitutional amendment, has acquired a visibility, specificity, and articulation only because of the "citizens' constitution" perspective that received formal expression in 1982. The contrast of each with the other highlights their distinctive assumptions, as well as the magnitude of the task confronting those who would build bridges between them. They structure the Canadian community in different ways, and thus in their constitutional coexistence they send contradictory answers to the citizen's query, "What is the constitution's answer to the question, 'Who am I?'"

The amending formula defines Canada as a country of governments presiding over and speaking for the national and provincial communities that federalism sustains. Its implicit assumption is that only the cleavages defined by federalism have to be catered to in the amending formula, and they can be represented by governments. The Charter, however, defines Canadians as a single community of rights-bearers, makes only limited concessions to provincialism,[8] and clearly engenders a non-deferential attitude toward those who wield government power. The community message of the Charter contradicts the community message of the amending formula. The Charter, in addition to defining Canadians in terms of rights, also singles out specific categories for particular recognitions and rights – women, official-language minorities, multicultural Canadians, and others. By so doing, it states that the federal-provincial cleavage, and the communities derived from it, do not exhaust the constitutionally significant identities that Canadians now possess. Succinctly, the Charter states what the amending formula denies, that "federalism is not enough" – that Canadians are more than a federal people.

A contemporary Lord Durham visiting Canada would identify two visions warring in the bosom of the same constitution. For evidence, the observer need only look at the recent controversy over both the process and substance of the Meech Lake constitutional amendments. The Meech Lake attempt to employ the amending formula as a vehicle to resolve a problem in the governments' constitution – described by the official actors, especially by Ottawa, as the absence of Quebec's government from the constitutional family – foundered because the various diverse constituencies linked to the Charter were unwilling to accept their exclusion from the process of constitution-making or to accept any weakening of the Charter. As Samuel LaSelva observes, the Charter's contribution is to pay attention to our existence as individuals and members of groups that resist being confined in the categories of federalism. Federalism "lacks the conceptual resources" to respond to the claims of individuals and groups for freedom and justice: "That is why a Bill of Rights is so important in a federal state. Through it, individuals and groups are given recognition in a federal system, and their interests are placed on the same footing as those of other constitutional actors."[9] That recognition, and that same footing, however, do not extend to the amending formula. Meech Lake, accordingly, became an arena within which these competing visions confronted each other, although not all the contestants would agree with the way I have characterized Meech Lake in chapter 4.

If this monograph underlines tensions, ambiguities, and dilemmas at the heart of our constitutional existence, rather than a safe harbour at journey's end, it nevertheless portrays where we now are. However, since our present location is not an equilibrium position, Canadians will soon need some appropriate prescriptions about what is to be done. For one set of essays, however, I hope that *diagnosis* of the problem is as much as can be expected.

I AM CONSCIOUS THAT I have not been giving federalism the pride of place it customarily receives in constitutional discussions and that Quebec has not loomed over every page as the focal point of whatever

constitutional problems Canadians are experiencing. If federalism
and Quebec are not given their proper due in the first three chapters
of this book, the reasons are threefold. First, the constitutional
importance of federalism, and the significance of Quebec within it,
are proclaimed by armies of commentators, by the weight of tradition, and by the role of governments in shaping constitutional debate;
to some extent, therefore, my stance is a minor corrective to a much
more powerfully entrenched bias. Second, and related, there is no
doubt an element of onesidedness involved in the attempt to stake
out a position that is not part of the conventional wisdom, especially
in political science circles. I believe that the Charter represents a more
pronounced change in our constitutional culture than we generally
appreciate. My judgment is not universally shared, either by my colleagues or by our governors. Indeed, the latter clearly acted on contrary assumptions when they attempted to respond to a problem in
federalism via Meech Lake as if the Charter had never happened.
Third, to live in Vancouver – where one can look across the Pacific
toward Asia, where one in seven of the population is a visible minority, and where in many schools more than 50 per cent of the student
population has English as a second language – is to catch a glimpse
of the Canadian future in which duality, founding peoples, the Plains
of Abraham, British constitutional traditions, and the cleavages of
federalism have diminished credibility as constitutional sign-posts.

The latter factors are obviously not archaeological survivals from
a vanished civilization, for they relate to still vital aspects of our present situation, and they are embedded in our institutional and constitutional arrangements, as well as in our political and intellectual
traditions. They have powerful defenders. They will, however, have
to accommodate to the new realities of ethnic, racial, and cultural
pluralism that cannot be rolled back and that represent the Canadian
version of global phenomena. We have to grapple with what L.S.
Lustgarten, referring to the changed ethnic demography of Western
states, described as "irreversible ... [and] the dominant characteristic
of twentieth-century states: ethnic pluralism within the framework of
a united polity."[10] In constitutional terms, much of our grappling will
occur via the Charter and the language of rights it fosters. Accordingly, what we now are, and should be, in constitutional and other
terms can no longer be answered by looking to our origins.

If the reader detects in this book a relative shortfall in the
presentation of what is well known, and an implicit and explicit
underlining of an orientation I believe is underestimated and underappreciated, I plead guilty. In extenuation, I can point to publications
of my former self, when I could not be accused of underestimating

the significance of federalism and its governments.[11] Indeed, those who are so inclined can attack my present incarnation with my previous incarnation, a situation I may find difficult to handle because I may be a triumphant winner and crestfallen loser at the same time.

In any event, chapter 4, "The Lessons of Meech Lake," brings the federalism dimension of governments, of Quebec, and of the amending formula together with the rights-oriented culture generated by the Charter. In that chapter, the federal-provincial and Quebec-and-the-rest-of-Canada aspects of our existence are given the tribute of attention they normally receive automatically when the constitution is discussed. The chapter, however, makes clear that their traditional hegemony as the basic concerns of the written constitution is now challenged. Canada's future constitutional health will depend on the answer given to that challenge.

CHAPTER ONE

International Influences on the Charter

We do not suffer from an absence of interpretations of how the Constitution Act, 1982, came into being. Bourgeois and Marxist scholars, insiders and outsiders, axe-grinders and axe-sharpeners, aboriginals, feminists, and others – categories with overlapping membership – show no signs of fatigue as they swell the introspective literature. While much of the analysis that explores and interprets the great events Canadians have lived through – our "blooding" as a nation, our coming of age – is impressive, we lack those dispassionate, exhaustive accounts that only the passing of time might allow.

We are still too close to the tumultuous events of the last three decades to write confidently of their larger meaning in our evolution as a people. The formal amendments in 1982 have only begun to restructure the working of our constitutional order in directions that remain unclear. These circumstances drive interpretation toward prescription in an effort to influence a future that has not yet jelled.

It is not, however, only the recency of the Constitution Act that ensures that academic and political controversy will attend its interpretation for the foreseeable future, but also its enduring significance for future generations. When suitably interpreted, such events can be employed as weapons in the ongoing conflict among rival groups for present and future advantage. Interpretation of the Constitution Act, accordingly, will be no more a matter of indifference to the partisan competitors of the coming decades than was the meaning to be affixed to the Durham Report, the BNA Act of 1867, the hanging of Louis Riel, or the battle on the Plains of Abrahams more than two centuries ago. The long-lasting and irresolute debate over the compact theory of Confederation confirms that such intellectural disagreements are kept alive more by the cleavages on which they feed than by irreconcilable differences of a purely scholarly nature.

Duplessis's advocacy of the compact theory derived not from his historical naïveté, as some English-Canadian critics of the theory appeared to believe, but from the theory's utility for his provincialist objectives.

Given these political and academic realities, my purposes here are limited. I hope only to modify slightly the angle of vision that we bring to bear on our recent constitutional evolution. In this chapter I shall argue that selective myopia has biased our understanding of the Charter's emergence – specifically, that the role of international factors in stimulating the Charter project has been seriously underestimated.

Unfortunately, the division of academic labour within political science has traditionally separated the study of domestic politics and international politics. Fortunately, this division has been challenged recently from two directions – by the growth of interest in the domestic sources of foreign policy and by its converse, the study of the international sources of domestic cleavages and policy. The latter is lucidly summed up by Gourevitch in language that I have tried to take to heart: "The international system is not only a consequence of domestic politics and structures but a cause of them ... International relations and domestic politics are therefore so interrelated that they should be analyzed simultaneously as wholes."[1]

THE INTERNATIONAL ENVIRONMENT

Interpretations of our recent constitutional discontents have focused overwhelmingly on domestic factors. Demands and responses, inputs and outputs, have been conceived in an insular fashion, almost as if Canadians inhabited a separate planet under their total control, and so minimal attention has been paid to our location in an international network of states and peoples.

Admittedly, various particulars external to Canada are commonly noted, such as the inescapable involvement of the United Kingdom's government in patriation, the intervention of General de Gaulle with his "Vive le Québec libre" declamation, and the international dimensions of the feminist movement. Although these and other external phenomena are singly drawn to our attention, they are depicted as isolated, random influences that affected only marginally a constitutional struggle driven overwhelmingly by domestic dynamics.

It would be perverse and unconvincing to deny the indigenous factors behind the Québécois nationalism, western discontent, and aboriginal grievances that shattered our former consensus or to argue that the road to the Constitution Act, with its Charter, was not influenced at every stage by the inherited arenas of federalism and parliamentary government within which we battled. However, to attribute significance to domestic factors is an academic commonplace that requires no underlining. In contrast, the pervasive international dimension to our struggles has received little concentrated attention. I propose to highlight that dimension, with specific reference to the Charter, precisely because it has been underappreciated. I hope that the counterbias of my approach will be salutary, given the disproportionate weighting conventionally attributed to domestic forces.

Domestic actors often derived meaning, identities, resources, and purposes from the international arena. The very definition of statehood evolved, as did the criteria appropriate to the evaluation of citizen-state relations, as the explosion of new states and new peoples onto the world stage convulsed the international system in recent decades. Ethnicity acquired an unanticipated domestic salience among formerly quiescent minorities in the Western world with the dissolution of the international racial hierarchies on which European imperialisms had been based. Belsen, Buchenwald, and the Gulag Archipelago seared their message of inhumanity into our chastened understanding that the state could be the greatest enemy, exploiter, and tyrant of its own peoples.

At the same time as these recognitions lifted the scales from our eyes, the post–Second World War international trading system under GATT drew its member states, including Canada, into tighter bonds of global economic interdependence. Concurrently, the striking growth of international organizations, both governmental and nongovernmental, underlined the limited capacity of the divided state system to grapple with political, economic, and ecological interdependence. Some scholars, observing these tendencies, along with the growing power of the multinational corporation, predicted the impending demise of the historic state system battered by an emergent, engulfing internationalism. The more modest perspective of this chapter asserts simply that individual states and their peoples respond, in both domestic and foreign policies, to an environment composed of other states and peoples. Skocpol appropriately reminds us "of the various ways in which state structures and actions are conditioned by historically changing transnational contexts. These contexts impinge on individual states through geopolitical relations of interstate domination and competition, through the international communication of ideals and models of public policy, and through world economic patterns of trade, division of productive activities, investment flows, and international finance. States necessarily stand at the intersections between domestic socio-political orders and the transnational relations within which they must maneuver for survival and advantage in relation to other states. The modern state as we know it ... has always been, since its birth in European history, part of a system of competing and mutually involved states."[2]

We need little reminder, especially in Canada, of the extent to which domestic economies are internationalized by their links with the global economy. We are less sensitive to the extent to which domestic societies, in matters other than economic, are similarly internationalized by links with the global society of peoples external to their borders. In Canada, these international societal links are structured by a rapidly changing domestic ethnic demography that, by the 1981 census, included over seventy "well-defined" ethnic groups.[3] As a by-product, the tensions and cleavages of many homelands are often reproduced in our midst. More generally, according to Oran Young, "the contemporary period has witnessed growing shifts in the patterns of human attention, information, and expectations which have had the effect of increasing the impact of events occurring all over the world on internal activities within the individual units of the system. Fashions both in patterns of consumption and in political attitudes, for example, now spread rapidly across national boundaries on a popular as well as elite basis ... There has been a movement away from parochialism in the perceptual horizons of broad segments of the world's population."[4]

Accordingly, although some scholars are unconvinced, there seems to have been a decline in psychological autarchy, especially among the citizens of democracies. At least with respect to the movement of values and ideas, any view of the state as a "relatively hard-shelled unit"[5] seems out of date.

State élites are subject to pervasive pressures from the international state system to respond to new norms of state behaviour and citizens' entitlement. The moral crusade against the racial practices of the Union of South Africa provides the kind of compelling contemporary evidence that is less visible in countries such as Canada, whose behaviour is in reasonable accord with applicable international norms. Logically, of course, that sensitive Canadian empathy to international cues, evident in the evolution of the Charter idea, confirms the domestic impact of external factors more fully than does South African resistance, until very recently, to the international assault on apartheid.

A strong version of my thesis would claim that the Charter was the direct result of systemic international factors, that the cues and pressures from the international environment inexorably pulled citizens and elites in the direction of certain emergent requirements of statehood. A very weak version would attribute only a trivial, contextual, decorative significance to external factors. As my argument proceeds, it will become clear that I see international pressures and incentives as inducing, conditioning, and influencing, rather than controlling or determining. This position, however, is not intended to downgrade international factors, for my assessment of domestic factors is the same. The state possesses a limited autonomy, and political and bureaucratic élites are not without choice. That autonomy and that choice are exercised in contexts of opportunity and constraint that derive from both international and domestic factors. Part of the domestic constraint derives from the citizenry, subject, like governments, to the conditioning of international forces. Further, citizens have resources which, in a democracy, they employ in the expectation that their voices will be heard. The government's monopoly of force is countered by the capacity of citizens to award or withhold the gift of legitimacy to the state and its office holders. In Western democracies, the criteria governing the bestowal of that gift have been pervasively influenced in recent decades by an internationally derived consciousness of rights that subtly moulded perceptions of both state élites and ordinary citizens of the norms that should govern their relations.

Whatever utility attends my efforts to expand on the preceding paragraphs will depend on the success with which a catalogue of fairly well-known particulars can be drawn together into a pattern that makes sense. Only a convincing interpretive framework can give life to what, in its absence, will be no more than an aggregation of individual items.

THE EROSION OF BRITISHNESS

Few aspects of our recent constitutional evolution are more dramatic than the repudiation of the principle and practice of parliamentary supremacy by the adoption of the Charter of Rights and Freedoms. While the existence of the override in section 33 – which allows Parliament or a provincial legislature to declare that an act in whole or part shall operate notwithstanding its conflict with section 2 or sections 7 to 15 of the Charter – qualifies that repudiation, the override, a constrained and weak expression of the parliamentary supremacy that was central to our constitutional tradition for more than a century, appears to have little of the legitimacy of the Charter itself, so recently arrived. To a large extent, of course, the Charter's legitimacy reflects the international mobilization of support for charters and bills of rights, particularly by the United Nations, which is discussed below. The ultimate triumph of the Charter in Canada, however, also reflected a parallel decline in support for parliamentary supremacy. The socio-intellectual history of that decline remains unwritten, and my explanation, accordingly, will be somewhat speculative. It was not, however, simply the converse of growing support for entrenched rights. Nor can the decline be explained solely by recourse to domestic developments.

For the Fathers of Confederation, parliamentary responsible government was a positive heritage that differentiated Canada from the United States and gratifyingly confirmed the evolutionary nature of Canadian constitutional development. In the eloquent language of Alexander Brady, "The consequences of the triumph of responsible government are many, but one commands particular attention. Canadians could henceforth feel confident that the essential fabric of the British constitution was their own acquisition, secured through their persistent advocacy, fitted to their peculiar circumstances, and fostered as the substance and symbol of their political identity in North America."[6] In the post-1945 period, the status of parliamentary government in Canada was weakened by the relative decline of the country of its origin – as a world power, as a centre of empire, and as an economic leader. That decline, as John Holmes observed, was not immediately apparent. Britain, sustained by the "aura of a great power," still loomed large in the calculations of Canadian policy-makers into the 1950s.[7] In the 1960s and 1970s, however, economic malaise gave birth to a negative international image, captured in the phrase "the British disease." Declining global power gave impetus to centrifugal nationalism in Scotland and Wales which challenged the image of political stability long associated with the British political tradition.

The weakening of Canadian identification with the United Kingdom to which these developments contributed was reinforced by the diminution in economic links between Canada and the United Kingdom. According to the Macdonald Commission, plummeting Canadian-British trade figures reflected the triumph of "North American geography ... over the British economic connections derived from our colonial origins in the British Empire. The National Policy of 1879, designed to integrate us on an East/West basis and supplemented by later imperial preference to link us with British markets, is now but a shadow of its former self ... Britain, a much weaker power now than when we began our Canadian journey in 1867, has joined the European Community. Our trade with Britain is much reduced from earlier times: it represented 2.2 percent of our merchandise exports and 2.5 percent of our merchandise imports in 1984, well under half of our growing trade with Japan. The United States is now overwhelmingly dominant as our major trading partner."[8]

British parliamentary supremacy no longer seemed so central to Canadian identity as the prestige and status associated with connection to the United Kingdom eroded. Although as late as the 1950s, opposition to a growing support for a Canadian Bill of Rights could still be justified in terms of defending our British heritage, and by tarring a Bill of Rights with the stigma of Americanism,[9] by the 1970s such arguments appeared strained. By the time of the 1980–1 Special Joint Committee of the Senate and of the House of Commons on the Constitution of Canada, dealing with the proposed constitutional resolution to be transmitted to Westminster, the remaining defenders of parliamentary supremacy were clearly in retreat. The dominant thrust of the interveners was to strengthen the Charter. The once-imperial mother had lost the capacity to bestow sanctity on the parliamentary institutions that had been her most important nineteenth-century constitutional gift to her Canadian subjects. By this time, of course, the considerable British interest in a Bill of Rights for the United Kingdom could only confirm the propriety of questioning the continuing virtues of parliamentary supremacy in the Canadian context.

The shifting ethnic demography of Canada made an independent contribution to the erosion of support for parliamentary supremacy. At Confederation, about 60 per cent of the population of the new nation was of British origin; by the 1940s this had dipped below 50 per cent; it will almost certainly drop below 40 per cent in the near future, and its continuing shrinkage is virtually guaranteed by the pattern of immigration. This relative decline is the by-product of the increasing proportion of the Canadian population that is of neither British nor French extraction, growing from about 8 per cent at the time of Confederation, to about one-third of the Canadian population in the 1981 census, to 38 per cent by the 1986 census.[10] Further, within the last few decades the composition of immigrants has changed dramatically, from approximately 80 per cent from countries with a European heritage to almost three-quarters from Asia, Africa, Latin America, and the Caribbean. Almost half of Canadian immigration now comes from Asia. Between 1971 and 1986 the numbers of Canadians who had been born in Africa, Asia, and Latin America grew by 340 per cent.[11] One scholar projects a Canadian visible minority population, excluding aboriginals, of almost 10 per cent early in the next century, nearly double the 5.6 per cent of the population that it comprised in 1986.[12]

This ethnic transformation unquestionably attenuates the historic supportive link between ethnicity and a "a Constitution similar in Principle to that of the United Kingdom." British Canada, defined by culture, history, and positive links to the United Kingdom, has been replaced by anglophone Canada, united by language, but ever more heterogeneous in terms of race, ethnicity, religion, culture, origins, and historical memories. Consequently, as Breton argues, "building a British-type of society is not a legitimate agenda anymore."[13] The link between language and constitutional Britishness that had held for an earlier British Canada was sundered for the later anglophone Canada that succeeded it. Concurrently, anglophone Canada had to readjust to the enhanced status of the French language in Canada and of Quebec in the Canadian federal system.

Many of the new post-war immigrants, whose numbers steadily reduced the numerical significance of the two founding European peoples, came from motherlands where the trusting attitude to the state implicit in the British parliamentary tradition would have been a mark of naïveté. Many of the visible minorities had little prior experience with constitutional government, British or other. As minorities, fearful of being singled out for negative treatment, they were naturally drawn toward the idea of judicially entrenched rights and away from parliamentary majoritarianism, whose deficiencies were less visible to those likely to wield majority power.

From a different perspective, a recurring argument in the early post-war years was that the influx of new immigrants of varying cultural and political backgrounds invalidated the historical belief that respect for rights could be left to a "natural," virtually automatic socialization into the British heritage. This trust in the implicit educative powers of tradition, aside from its questionable applicability to French Canada, did not extend to many of the new immigrants, for whom the educative effect of a visible written code was considered essential.

More generally, as will be noted below, the growing percentage of Canadians of neither British nor French background challenged a constitutional discourse that gave privilege to duality and appeared to grant diminished recognition and status to late arrivals. Self-interest dictated the latter's antipathy to constitutional assumptions that stressed origins, foundings, the British and French peoples, and the constitution which the latter had built in their own image. Thus immigration-induced demographic change diminished the legitimacy granted by its British origins to the inherited written and unwritten constitution and challenged the French-English entente that ran through post-Confederation constitutional history.

Growing support for a Charter in Canada was facilitated by removal of specific impediments. In this connection, the abolition of appeals to the Judicial Committee of the Privy Council in 1949 made a little-noticed indirect contribution to the lessening of support for parliamentary supremacy and to the provision of a positive environment in which Charter support could more easily grow.

The Judicial Committee's location at the apex of the judicial hierarchy from 1867 to 1949 had consequences for Canadian constitutional evolution that go beyond its controversial impact on Canadian federalism. The successful nationalist attack on the Judicial Committee, a body that had been eulogized up to the Depression for the quality of its jurisprudence and as a link of empire, not only made the Supreme Court of Canada truly supreme but precipitated a search for an indigenous Canadian jurisprudence which was now seen to have been stifled by the long subordination to British law-lords.[14]

That search generated receptivity to the international pressure for a Charter that emerged soon after the war. Part of the explanation for growing Canadian interest in and support for a Charter, therefore, is structural. Advocacy of a Bill of Rights presupposed an autonomous Canadian judicial system and thus was politically incompatible with the domiciling of ultimate judicial power over the Canadian constitution in London. Charter interpretation, with its uniquely necessary sensitivity to local conditions and Canadian values, could not be handed over to an alien court. There is a sense, therefore, in which the pre-1949 dominance of the Judicial Committee sustained parliamentary supremacy by inhibiting development of a Charter movement in Canada. Conversely, removal of this structural impediment cleared the way for a more positive appreciation of entrenched rights at a time when the general erosion of the British complexion of the constitution was generating efforts to root it more firmly in indigenous conditions. It may also be speculated that, as the monarchy came to play a diminished role in Canadian constitutional symbolism as Britain receded from Canadian consciousness and as Canadians were appointed governors-general, constitutional theories based on deference to élites were harder to sustain. As freedom no longer wore a crown, and as legitimacy was seen no longer as descending from above but as proceeding from the mass democracy, diffusion of rights consciousness encountered reduced resistance.

More generally, nationalist support for a Bill of Rights in the 1950s was part of the historic colony-to-nation movement that had propelled successive steps in Canadian independence from Great Britain. In contrast to the overtly political purpose of constraining centrifugal pressures that drove the federal government's support for a Charter in the late 1960s and the 1970s, the earlier support had "less to do with leashing the provinces and more to do with the evolution of the symbolic basis of the Canadian Constitution from the authority of the British Parliament to that of the people of Canada."[15]

The intellectual background to the constitutional introspection of recent decades in Canada is incomplete, therefore, if it does not encompass the underlying shift in basic constitutional assumptions that attended the drifting apart of Canada and the United Kingdom. For the generation of English-Canadian political scientists born before the First World War, the revered centrepiece of the Canadian constitutional tradition had been responsible parliamentary government. Alexander Brady, for example, saw Canada as firmly rooted in its British past, while R.M. Dawson took great pride in "the priceless political heritage which Canada has received from England."[16]

For the next generation of scholars, however, the United Kingdom lost its intellectual centrality. The social sciences and law increasingly derived inspiration from the United States. Bagehot, Bryce, and Dicey no longer graced the research footnotes of the professional students of Canadian politics who became prominent in the 1960s and 1970s. By this time, scholars and politicians scanning the international landscape for possible reforms to patch up or heal a threatened constitutional order seldom looked to the United Kingdom for inspiration. For advocates of electoral reform, the "British" system employed by Canadians was contrasted unfavourably with foreign systems of proportional representation; Senate reformers often looked to West Germany; and the ombudsman role of citizen defender originated in Scandinavia. While the Charter had diffuse international roots as well as the next-door American example, these influences and models all testified to the supplementing of a derivative British constitutionalism in Canada with a more cosmopolitan set of influences.

Even the British two-party system, long praised as a role model for Canadian parties,[17] subsequently lost its appeal in Canada, partly of course because it no longer was an accurate description of the British scene. In addition, however, various Canadian scholars now identified serious deficiencies in the Canadian party system which, by the mechanism of party discipline, seemed to frustrate regional expression and thus weaken the legitimacy of the central government. Further, the party system, as conditioned by the electoral system, could no longer be counted on to produce nation-wide governing parties, a shortcoming that was believed to foster alienation in provinces/ regions deprived of significant representation on the government side of the House of Commons. Virtually all the solutions proposed involved departures from an idealized British-type two-party system that had captivated Canada's English-speaking intelligentsia, especially on the left, since the 1930s.

The relaxation of the British grip on Canadian constitutional identity was manifest in the great burst of nationalist activity in the years just after the war. This included the Canadian Citizenship Act (in 1947); admission of Newfoundland, abolition of appeals to the Judicial Committee, and domestication of part of the amending formula in Canada (all in 1949); and appointment of the first Canadian-born governor-general (in 1952). In the 1960s, following a long debate, the adoption of the maple leaf flag signalled the sundering of one more symbolic link with the United Kingdom.

These developments reflected and stimulated a psychological and cultural distancing on both sides. On the British side, that distancing derived from the implicit downgrading of the Commonwealth as the British moved toward Europe and finally joined the European Community. On the Canadian side, for reasons already noted, it reflected the diminishing relevance of the British connection and a concomitant loss of constitutional status for the parliamentary side of the Canadian wedding of federalism and parliamentary government. This decline symbolized a more general decomposition of constitutional Britishness and at least suggested that much of the previous constitutional tradition had been held together by the British identity that Canadians, especially English Canadians, had proudly brought to its evaluation.

In a separate development, francophone Québécois, little inclined to revere the British connection or the Westminster tradition, lost one of their few positive British links with the abolition of appeals to the Judicial Committee, a court they thought had well served the cause of Quebec and provincialism.

The capacity of parliamentary government to sustain a sense of Canadian distinctiveness in North America was conditioned by time and circumstance. It appears in retrospect that the traditional, positive evaluation of parliamentary government, unconstrained by entrenched rights, was intimately linked to the status of the United Kingdom as a great power and to the related tendency for many English Canadians to define themselves as British as long as significant domestic prestige continued to flow from the British connection. As that connection lost its instrumental value, Canadian support for the constitutional theory of parliamentary supremacy was weakened, along with a cluster of values, intellectual orientations, and practices that had previously given the Canadian constitution, and commentary on it, a distinctly British cast. By 1982, when patriation occurred, the residual British role in the amending process had only the support of inertia. For Trudeau, and few would have disagreed, it was devoid of any constitutional rationale, a leftover constitutional appendix from a previous era. One by one, the cluster of links between Canada and the United Kingdom, of which it earlier had been only a part, had fallen away, including the culturally transmitted bias in favour of parliamentary government.

The weakened appreciation for this formerly potent symbol of Canadian constitutional identity created a gap in the constitutional symbolism of an almost completely autonomous nation. The Charter that emerged to fill that gap brought entrenched rights, judicial supremacy, and a greatly enhanced role for the written portion of the constitution – all of which further distanced Canadians from their British constitutional origins.

From the 1950s to the 1980s, the declining allegiance to the British parliamentary side of Canadian political life coincided with selective interest in and positive appraisal of American constitutional theory and practice. This Canadian interest had two main roots. The first was the by-product of Canadian judicial autonomy, achieved in 1949. The ongoing task of umpiring a federal system, along with growing support for constitutionally entrenched rights, manifested initially in John Diefenbaker's weak Canadian Bill of Rights of 1960, and much more decisively in the 1982 Charter, made it inevitable that the US Supreme Court and American jurisprudence would acquire a practical prominence for Canadian scholars and practitioners that they had previously lacked.

Canadian constitutional scholarship became more comparative with growing emphasis on American scholarship and experience, as in the writings of Edward McWhinney,[18] or sought to incorporate American legal/constitutional theory into Canadian jurisprudence, as with Lyon and Atkey's *Canadian Constitutional Law in a Modern Perspective*.[19] This American thrust was stimulated by the US Supreme Court's leadership in breaking down segregation and by the court's liberal policy activism, especially under Chief Justice Earl Warren.

The second root which enhanced Canadian appreciation of American constitutional practice sprang from the efforts of Canadian scholars to uncover a structural reason for the constitutional malaise that was generating seemingly irresistible pressures for decentralization. Smiley's intrastate analysis of federalism, which argued that the crucial flaw in Canadian constitutional arrangements was the inability of the central government to represent, accommodate, and tame territorial particularisms, gained considerable support.[20] Subsequent scholarship, most notably by Roger Gibbins,[21] often saw the American congressional system, with its absence of tight party discipline, as greatly facilitating interregional brokerage and thus strengthening the central government within which such bargaining occurred.[22]

Thus, resurgent (and, to some, threatening) provincialism stimulated Canadian interest in the capacity for regional accommodation of American congressional arrangements. Shifting and flexible congressional coalitions appeared to mobilize legislative support with much greater sensitivity to regional concerns than was possible with the Canadian version of the British practice of party discipline. Concurrently, the emergence of a more demanding rights consciousness, and the possible utility of a Charter as an instrument of national integration, enhanced the visibility of the American Supreme Court as a model to which Canadian judges and constitutional scholars could look discriminatingly for insights into the future they might confront. Both of these developments made the practice and theory of American constitutionalism more, and that of the United Kingdom less, relevant to the constitutional choices confronting Canadians than had hitherto been the case.

INTERNATIONAL SOURCES OF POLITICIZED ETHNICITY

The society to which the 1982 Charter was a response had undergone a profound transformation since the Second World War. That change was many-sided, but for our purposes its chief characteristic was a dramatic escalation of nationalism and ethnicity that affected not only francophones but also those who fell outside the charmed category of "founding peoples." They in turn came to be divided into those primarily of European descent, at whom the 1971 policy of multiculturalism was initially directed, and the visible minorities whose situation was assessed in *Equality Now: Report of the Special Committee on Visible Minorities in Canadian Society* (1984). Concurrent with the progression from bilingualism to multiculturalism to multiracialism, the hitherto quiescent aboriginal peoples struggled to achieve a constitutional and practical recognition commensurate with their self-description as the First Nations of Canada.

Since 1945, a continuing stream of government policy and official inquiries has tried to come to grips with the ethnic pluralism that none had predicted in the inter-war years. From this perspective,

Diefenbaker and Trudeau share a similar pan-Canadianism, which they sought to strengthen in order to contain centrifugal pressures. From the Citizenship Act of 1947, to the Bill of Rights of 1960, the Official Languages Act of 1969, the official policy of multiculturalism in 1971, and the Charter of Rights of 1982, which gives constitutional recognition to ethnic and linguistic diversity, the Canadian state has been continuously grappling with the complexities of an ethnically heterogeneous society. The domestic politicization of ethnicity to which these state measures are responses and sometimes stimulants is fed by international forces, to which I now turn.

The ending of European empires and the resultant explosion of new states in Africa and Asia constituted decisive rejection of the ideology and practice of racial hierarchies based on a presumed European superiority. Settler communities in Kenya, Southern Rhodesia, Mozambique, Angola, and Algeria succumbed to indigenous nationalisms. The United Nations was transformed from a primarily European club to an unwieldy aggregation of more than 150 member states, many of which are small and poor, and most of which are non-white. For the last half-century, the international system has been responding to the impact of the Third World, whose non-European members struggle to overcome the insult and humiliation they experienced when, in an earlier era, they were "measured against a foreign standard of 'civilization' and ... found wanting."[23] The home populations of former imperial powers, such as Holland, Belgium, France, and the United Kingdom, were decisively pushed in a multiracial direction by the arrival of large numbers of their former colonial subjects. The emergence of new states, often accompanied by civil disorder, led to extensive population displacements, the creation of millions of refugees, and resultant moral and political pressure on Western democracies to open their frontiers to the homeless and dispossessed.

These changes in the international environment, in the global relationship between states and ethnic groups, profoundly affected the contemporary system of states. Woodrow Wilson's ideal of one ethnic nationality/one state has turned out to be an unattainable goal for most of the world's peoples. According to a recent writer, there are around 3,000 ethnic or tribal groups conscious of their separate identities. Well over 90 per cent of the world's over 150 sovereign states are multi-ethnic in composition.[24] As a result, the fond assumption that modernity would bid goodbye to ethnicity and regionalism, and usher in the triumph of class politics, has once more been put off to a distant future.

This unpredicted world of race and ethnic nationalism has altered the ethnic composition, cleavage structure, and politics of many Western societies, including Canada. Succinctly, the ending of racial hierarchies in the international system eroded the legitimacy of their domestic counterparts. The demise of colonialism precipitated Third World attacks on other surviving examples of racially based segregation and discrimination that had been its hallmark. In particular, the availability of the UN forum greatly enhanced the capacity of Third World countries to attack surviving racialist doctrines that had formerly justified their subordination to European imperial powers. In Jackson's pointed summation, after referring to the UN Charter, the Universal Declaration of Human Rights, and the UN Covenants on Human Rights, "Racial equality has been installed as a universal value of the international community."[25]

The global ideology of racial equality stimulated by this resurgent ethnicity has increased interethnic and interracial contacts as a by-product of the liberalized immigration requirements it has fostered. In general, the significance of race as a category in international political thought invests its domestic treatment with international dimensions absent from many other policy areas – hence, the tendency for Canadian aboriginals to scan the international environment for political resources that can be exploited for domestic purposes.

A host of international conventions, covenants, resolutions, and treaties provides international legitimacy to the principle of non-discrimination on grounds of race. As early as 1945, in *Re Drummond Wren*, Mr Justice Mackay of the Ontario High Court relied on the UN Charter, the Atlantic Charter, and other domestic and international evidence to strike down a restrictive land covenant barring the selling of land to "Jews, or to persons of objectionable nationality."[26] The ethnic and racial restrictions in Canadian franchise laws against Chinese, Japanese, East Indians, and Doukhobors were eliminated after 1945. In 1960, status Indians, who had previously been denied the franchise on the ground of its alleged incompatibility with their perceived wardship status, received the vote. "In postwar Canada," comment Carty and Ward, "newly ascendent liberal views on race and ethnic relations challenged traditional biases in electoral law, and, in response, governments dismantled these barriers one by one."[27]

Canada's aspirations to leadership in the multiracial Commonwealth, which replaced the empire and its white dominions, enhanced the country's exposure to the new egalitarian ideologies. In 1952, a plea by John Diefenbaker for the elimination of domestic racial discrimination was linked to Canada's membership in the Commonwealth, "with five to one of those who are members ... being of coloured races."[28] The resulting heightened sensitivity to racial discrimination posed a particular challenge to the historic assumptions that lay behind Canadian immigration policy.[29] As early as 1948, Indian officials informed the Canadian high commissioner in New Delhi that Canada's restrictive immigration policy was being used as an argument against India's membership in the Commonwealth. By the early 1950s, small numbers of Asians from the subcontinent were eligible for permanent residence in Canada – 150 from India, 100 from Pakistan, and 50 from Ceylon. Significantly, these modest relaxations are described as an "achievement of the External Affairs community" and of Lester Pearson.[30] Foreign ministers, R.J. Vincent recently argued, must "pay attention to human rights whether they like it or not," because they are caught in a network of "the conventions of positivist international law, by their explicit agreements and by custom and practice. This body of doctrine forms part of their social world."[31] In a more fundamental response in the 1960s to the changing international environment, Canadian immigration policy moved decisively from racially discriminatory toward universalistic criteria, and the resultant change in immigration patterns led to a more ethnically diverse society.

In general, the rhetoric and ideology of the emerging post-imperial international order reinforced ethnic and racial identities throughout the Western world and put on the defensive inequalities based on ascriptive criteria. The politicization of domestic cleavages, most obvious with respect to language, race, and ethnicity, also extended to the division between the sexes, to the disabled, to generational cleavages as youth emerged as a distinct category, and to multiple life-styles as sexual liberation movements extended the boundaries of the permissible and the legitimate. The movements behind the assertive self-confidence of these politicized social categories had an international component, a factor that explains their simultaneous emergence throughout the Western world. Diffusion of the new normative order was facilitated by the easy mobility of persons and ideas across national boundaries, especially in open societies.[32]

The example of numerous small and weak mini-states and dwarf nationalisms reduced the necessary population size and economic requisites for statehood. In effect, statehood was redefined and the criteria for its possession were greatly relaxed, as new international norms and practices established themselves. Thus one scholar, responding to the proliferation of new states with minuscule populations, whose existence would have been inconceivable to government leaders only half a century ago, categorically asserted that "there is no minimum size for a sovereign state."[33]

For concentrated nationalist groups, like the Québécois, this change heightened the possibility and desirability of independence

by the provision of examples and justifications that had no counterpart in the years from Confederation to the Second World War.
Under this new international dispensation, an independent Quebec
would instantly become a significant performer in the international
community of nations. As René Lévesque informed the French
Assemblée nationale in 1977, an independent Quebec would immediately "rank eleventh among more than 150 countries in per capita
income."[34]

These (especially ethnic) developments challenged the integrative
capacities of governments. Social cohesion became more problematic.
By 1986, visible minorities accounted for more than one in seven
residents of Vancouver and Toronto. In these cities and elsewhere,
English was a second language to large majorities of the student
population in many schools. More generally, as David Cameron
recently observed, the Canada of the future will contain "a few, vast
metropolitan centers which are riotously multicultural" and whose
hinterlands remain populated by "'old style' Canadians."[35] Where ethnic groups had a territorial basis and saw themselves as nations, as
in Quebec, the integrity of the citizenship nation was challenged. For
the Canadian federal government, the containment of Québécois
nationalism, the response to aboriginal demands, and the alleviation
of ethnic and racial tensions became central concerns of statecraft.
Selective recognition of diversity in a succession of policies, and the
bond of rights held in common, emerged as defensive strategies to
contain centrifugal tensions stimulated by the international environment.

The politicization of ethnicity put parliamentary institutions on the
defensive, generated an antipathy to majoritarianism, and increased
the attractiveness of an entrenched Charter. In addition to its manifest role in protecting rights, such a Charter might be a servant of
national unity by strengthening the symbolism and contents of a
common citizenship. It could also be viewed as a response to international norms of appropriate behaviour in citizen-state relations, in
the same way as modified trade practices were a response to GATT.

THE INTERNATIONAL RIGHTS DIMENSION

In 1968, Maxwell Cohen attributed the novel and dramatic Canadian
interest in "human rights" to transformed international and domestic
beliefs which had "altered totally beyond anything that could have
been imagined two decades before."[36] "Human rights," he continued,
"became ... within the past twenty years, an important piece of

'debating' language ... part of the political dialogue, part of the debating experience of peoples in all parts of the world, even those in affluent societies."[37]

The most influential catalyst of that transformed climate of Canadian and international opinion was the United Nations, one of whose purposes has been to foster respect for fundamental freedoms and human rights.[38] Its 1945 Charter, followed by the Universal Declaration of Human Rights, adopted as a unanimous resolution of the General Assembly in 1948, and subsequent international covenants on Civil and Political Rights and on Economic, Social and Cultural Rights have been influential in channelling and stimulating a "rights" debate in Canada. Within the United Nations, rights are institutionalized in the various committees that monitor the performance of states under various UN conventions, in particular committees of the General Assembly, and in the UN Secretariat.[39] These UN activities and the proliferation of international normative instruments reflect the "emergence of a cosmopolitan regime of human rights,"[40] linked to a growing body of nascent international law. The latter, in turn, has generated a host of rights-oriented non-governmental organizations, such as Amnesty International, that wield the power of investigation and publicity on behalf of particular causes.[41] The cumulative result is an extraordinarily high profile for "rights," both domestically and internationally.

Initial Canadian responses to the inclusion of rights in the UN Charter, and to the subsequent Universal Declaration, were distinctly lukewarm. Canadian officials asserted the superior protection of rights under the British tradition, which they rather smugly contrasted with American experience, and also stressed the constitutional limitations of federalism in which some rights pertained to matters under provincial jurisdiction.[42] Although the Special Joint Committee of the Senate and House of Commons of Canada on Human Rights and Fundamental Freedoms (1947–8) and the Special Committee of the Senate on Human Rights and Fundamental Freedoms (1950) were explicit responses to the requirement for an analysis of Canadian practice in the light of the Charter and the Universal Declaration, they did not result in a Canadian version of the Charter. Nevertheless, it was standard practice for advocates of a Canadian Bill of Rights from the late 1940s on to cite the UN Charter and the Universal Declaration in support of their position, and the 1950 Senate committee did recommend a statutory Canadian Declaration of Human Rights derived in significant part from the Universal Declaration and limited to federal jurisdiction.[43] Thirty years later, nearly all the civil liberties and human rights organizations that appeared before the Special Joint Committee of the Senate and of the House of Commons on the Constitution of Canada (1980–1) stressed Canadian obligations under UN international covenants. Human Rights Commissioner Gordon Fairweather, after citing various UN instruments, by means of which Canada has "increased her accountability to the world community" asserted that such obligations could not be met without an entrenched Charter binding on both orders of government.[44]

Law professor John Claydon identified Canada's international obligations as both "the necessary and pervasive context" surrounding the Charter's introduction and adoption and also the "direct inspiration" for strengthening amendments.[45] The deputy Minister of justice, Roger Tassé, clearly indicated the appropriateness of the courts employing Canada's international human rights obligations to interpret the Charter.[46]

The Charter, the Universal Declaration, and subsequent covenants not only provided domestic groups with a powerful rights rhetoric legitimated by its UN origins but also suggested the criteria by which performance could be judged. In a forum such as the United Nations, it was obviously politically preferable for a state to employ written instruments, such as a Charter, to confirm its formal compliance with its UN obligations, than to try and explain that a parliamentary regime might better protect rights than a regime with a hollow charter designed for external consumption. That same international pressure put federalism as well as parliamentary supremacy on the defensive: Canadian legislative response to international commitments requiring provincial action could not be undertaken by the federal government acting alone.[47]

Thus the direct and indirect proselytizing on behalf of rights by the United Nations challenged regimes practising federalism and employing parliamentary supremacy to modify their constitutional arrangements, as a Bill of Rights became an almost essential attribute of contemporary statehood. Accordingly, it is not surprising that a Bill of Rights has become virtually an automatic component of new constitutions, or that Bills of Rights have become increasingly comprehensive,[48] or that an established state such as Canada, that had long existed without an entrenched Charter, has recently introduced one, or that New Zealand is seriously considering doing so. In Australia, as well, a recent writer suggests, traditional British legal and constitutional assumptions are challenged by a "global [human rights] constituency."[49] That a number of new states have based their constitutions on the Universal Declaration of Human Rights provides additional testimony to the existence of an international rights regime.[50]

Even in the United Kingdom, a Bill of Rights has acquired influential advocates, including Lords Scarman and Hailsham, while Britain's membership in the European Community has made it subject to the European Convention. A Bill of Rights, asserted one of its prominent legal supporters, would identify the United Kingdom "with the strong and growing international movement for the protection of Human Rights," a rationale frequently employed by advocates of a Charter for Canada.[51] These developments lend force to the recent suggestion that one possible successor to the no-longer acceptable standard of (European) "civilization" as a source of international precepts or norms might be respect for human rights.[52]

new norms

The recent summary of a shrewd student of rights and the international system provides an appropriate conclusion to these comments: "There is now an area of domestic conduct in regard to human rights ... that is under the scrutiny of international law ... [This] expose[s] the internal regimes of all the members of international society to the legitimate appraisal of their peers. This may turn out not to have been a negligible change in international society."[53]

CONCLUSION

To analyse the 1982 Charter and the process from which it emerged in ignorance of the international dimension would be to exclude material essential to comprehensive understanding. The Charter of Rights is a legacy of the influence of international factors intertwining with domestic considerations.

First, the declining legitimacy of the constitutional theory of parliamentary supremacy in Canada is inexplicable without appreciating the constitutional distancing between Canada and the United Kingdom that accompanied the Canadian progress from "colony to nation" and the reduction of a formerly great imperial power, after the Second World War, to the status of a middle power beset with serious problems. Second, the separate emergence of a global ideology of human rights, and its institutionalized propagation by the United Nations, dramatically enhanced the visibility and legitimacy of entrenched charters as constitutional instruments. Third, and closely related to the second, ethnicity and race emerged as pervasive components of collective identity and political discourse in the post-imperial international order. The domestic spillovers in Canada included heightening of racial and ethnic identities, emergence of an independence-seeking nationalism in Quebec, and more liberal immigration requirements that further added to our ethnic heterogeneity.

Canadians were particularly susceptible to the enhanced international salience of race and ethnicity and to the vigorous international rights discourse because of the prominence they accorded to the Commonwealth and to the United Nations as arenas for action and as windows on the emergent international state system. Throughout this period, therefore, Canadians were readjusting their constitutional machinery and their public identities not in isolation from a global context that had its own shaping effect on conceptions of the desired relations between citizens and governments. "The functions that are viewed as proper and legitimate for the state," Krasner observed, "are influenced by general international norms and practices."[54]

The dialectic between governments and peoples does not take place in isolation from the ocean of states and nations in which both exist. Indeed, the very concepts of state and nation in different historical periods are evolutionary products of an international state system that does not stand still.

Through the last half-century, as in previous decades, Canadian first ministers and ordinary citizens responded to various developing norms of statehood. Trudeau avidly sought elimination of the embarrassing continuing amending responsibility of the British Parliament partly because of its vestigial incongruity in a world where the newest of the new states, small and poor as they were, had complete possession of a capacity that ancient Canada lacked. Both the independence-seeking nationalism of Quebec, and the idea and the reality of the Charter as an instrument to combat it, were stimulated by an international system in which small states were viable and charters were international symbols of modernity as well as instruments of national integration.

The very identities of citizens, and the values they brought to their role in constitutional politics, were shaped by international factors of which, especially in the case of group leaders, they were fully aware. The social movements that provided public support for a Charter virtually all had a significant international dimension. The feminist movement, aboriginal demands, gay and lesbian aspirations, and the claims of many other groups are incomprehensible without recognizing the significance of the international dimension in providing intellectual and emotional sustenance to the claimants, in providing them with the positive reinforcement that comes from the knowledge that one is not alone.

The constitutional struggle that convulsed us for two decades, the Constitution Act of 1982 that was the response, the decline of parliamentary supremacy, an entrenched Charter, an enhanced judicial role, the feminist movement, the political emergence of the aboriginal peoples, and multiculturalism are all linked in more than a trivial way to developments in the global context that interacted with domestic transformations in Canadian society. Thus, in responding to the new Canada that clashed with the inherited constitutional order, the federal government, as the leading actor in constitutional politics, was responding to the domestic effects of international forces. That a central component of its response was a Charter of Rights and Freedoms, an instrument that had been ceaselessly propagated in international forums, was not a historical accident.

To portray the Charter as in part the product of the tugs and pulls of the international system, as this chapter has done, is not to employ the language of determinism. As Gourevitch observes, the international system is underdetermining. Its effects can be weighed only after an examination of domestic politics and in full recognition that states and their leaders are not puppets, but choosers.[55] But the system of domestic pressures, especially if considered as having an existence independent of the incentives and disincentives offered by the external environment, is also inadequate and underdetermining. The delivery of that message, whether thin or portentous may be left to the reader to decide, has been the purpose of this chapter.

CHAPTER TWO

Constitutional Refashioning of Community

In a recent article, Charles Tilly observed that "the ends of wars make accessible to analysis relationships that are normally extremely hard to distinguish amidst the peace time play of interests and institutions: relationships among states, between citizens and states, among different segments of the same state."[1] The same can be said about a major constitutional crisis. It highlights relationships and patterns otherwise less visible.

The title of this chapter may appear vaguely disturbing, with its suggestion of deliberate manipulation of our identities in the service of some higher end. On reflection, however, it is evident that the making and unmaking of political communities are the quintessential political act. Such making and unmaking are an unending process as daily interactions between citizens and their governments subtly transform the meaning of citizenship, the boundaries of community, and the balance between rights and duties. Simultaneously, the international environment transmits its own evolving messages, clear at the core and obscure at the margins, of the contemporary attributes of statehood and what it means to be a political people.

Occasionally, these gradualist evolutionary tendencies, whose glacial movements are not always easy to detect, are disrupted by profound conflicts that remind us of the precariousness of our civic togetherness. These challenges to our continuity inspire policies that attempt to transcend the divisions that threaten our survival – or contrary policies that are directed to a political divorce. Since these conflicts and the efforts to resolve them are forcing grounds for rapid, intensive collective learning, they deserve more academic scrutiny than do events in less troubled eras. From this perspective, the Constitution Act, 1982, and particularly the Charter – responses to the most serious state-threatening challenge in Canadian history – justify the extended examination they have received from the scholarly community. In this chapter, I hope to add to that literature by unremitting focus on one dimension of major constitutional change – its community-shaping objectives. While this focus has not been ignored in the extant literature, there is a tendency for it to fade and be displaced by the detailed analysis of the fate of particular constitutional clauses as their meaning undergoes judicial refinement. So my angle of vision here represents an effort to keep alive perhaps the basic question of constitutional studies: in the Canadian case, the relation between constitutional choices and the kind of people(s) we become.

As a preliminary, a reminder of past examples to shape collective identities by constitutional instruments will help to set the stage for more recent efforts.

HISTORICAL BACKGROUND[2]

In his Report on the Affairs of British North America (1839), Lord Durham wrote scathingly of the backward, unprogressive character of French Canadians, "a people with no history, and no literature." He entertained "no doubts as to the national character which must be given to Lower Canada; it must be that of the British Empire; ... that of the great race which must, in the lapse of no long period of time, be predominant over the whole North American continent."[3] Durham advocated institutional engineering to submerge the distinctive nationality of French Canada within the framework of a united colony where the progressive, superior, commercial civilization of English Canada would overwhelm the less competitive culture of the habitant, to the benefit of both. Durham, according to David Cameron, recognized that constitutional reform, following on the recent rebellions, would be of little effect if it left "the elements of society unaltered." Thus the purpose of constitutionally uniting the two Canadas "was to compose Lower Canadian society differently ... He resolved the problem of two warring nations by dissolving one into the other."[4]

By the mid-1860s, the inadequacies of Durham's diagnosis, which had led to the merging of Lower and Upper Canada in the United Province of Canada in 1841, were evident in the continuing French-Canadian sense of nationality, the existence of aggressive French-Canadian leadership, the emergence of a rudimentary de facto federal system within the framework of the formally unitary colony, and the developing recognition of French-Canadian rights. By the early

1860s, the faltering political system of the United Province of Canada was becoming unworkable. A new arrangement was necessary.

In the competition between institutions and ethnicity, the latter had triumphed. In the next phase of constitutional craftsmanship – Confederation – the limitations of institutional engineering directed to the disappearance of French Canada induced a more sociological sensitivity to the enduring factor of national consciousness in the minority. Confederation was more respectful of French-English duality. Federalism in the 1867 act was designed to minimize ethnic competition between French and English by separating the united province of Canada into two provinces, Quebec and Ontario, to be dominated by French and English majorities respectively. Both communities thus escaped from the destructive interethnic competition of their recent past into provinces they separately controlled.

Confederation, however, was more than a response to and accommodation of ethnic linguistic duality, or of the colonial diversities in Atlantic Canada. In the same way as the Act of Union of 1840, it had major community-building tasks on its agenda. The highly centralist federal structure, which originally encompassed four provinces and added Manitoba in 1870, British Columbia in 1871, and Prince Edward Island in 1873, lacked the support of a national community at its inception. There were no Canadians in 1867, partly because, while the colonists were linked to a common British imperial authority, they had been politically shaped in separate colonies, with the partial exception of course of the Act of Union experience of the future citizens of Quebec and Ontario. Further, the élitist nature of the move to Confederation did little to develop identifications with the new country within the still colonial citizenry.

Canadians, accordingly, were a project for the future, not an inheritance from the past. They were to emerge as a result of the dominion government's successful performance of its responsibilities, including the essential nation-building tasks of territorial expansion, infrastructure development, and economic growth. From this perspective, the act of 1867 was a mobilizing instrument designed to create a new people whose historically based provincial identifications, derived from separate colonial pasts, were to be supplemented by developing identification with the new central government and the new Canadian community it was fostering. John A. Macdonald, as is well known, was confident that the provinces would become progressively insignificant in the not-too-distant future.

This, however, was not to be, for the BNA Act, 1867, as John Whyte recently reminded us, "contained an equally powerful idea, that of the federal division of legislative powers, which did match the diverse nature of Canada's communities."Macdonald's vision, he notes, "did not ... take. One can only assume that it did not match the economic, social and political reality."[5] The failure to "take," of course, was relative. The country survived. Canadians were created, and the result, 120 years later, is one of the oldest continuing political systems in the world. So this experiment in fashioning a community worked, albeit perhaps not as fully as some had hoped.

Our subsequent community history includes creation of two new provinces, Alberta and Saskatchewan in 1905, and the addition of Newfoundland as a tenth in 1949. In the former, two new provincial identities emerged in response to the de jure existence of the new jurisdictions created by drawing lines on a map. In the latter, a new Canadian identity emerged in response to the joining of Canada, while Newfoundlanders' sense of self, formerly that of an independent people, was reduced to a provincial identity.

Thus the country became more federal as it matured, growing from four provinces to ten provinces and two territories. The more than century-long dialectic of the interaction of the two orders of government with each other and with the societies and economies of an expanding Canada has been analysed in numerous scholarly accounts.

Both world wars of this century stimulated popular identifications with the central government in English Canada, heightened tensions between French and English, especially in the First World War, and strengthened provincial identifications in Quebec as French Canadians recoiled from the insensitivity of the other "founding people" to French Canadians' lesser psychological involvement in European wars. In the 1950s, an alleged nationalizing of sentiment among élites in the command posts of an interdependent society and economy was seen as portending inexorable centralization. Two decades later, apprehensive scholars in English Canada thought that the country was headed for breakup as a centrifugal provincialism, seemingly heedless of the larger community, threatened to fracture the Canadian collectivity. Most recently, of course, that fear was occasioned outside Quebec by the vigorous attempt of the Parti québécois to attain independence, the better to fashion its population into a single people. That dream, too, has been at least temporarily vanquished by the results of the Quebec referendum of 1980 and the subsequent constitutional settlement that Quebec's government refused to sign. Thus the relationship between the constitution and the Canadian and provincial communities has seldom dropped off our political and intellectual agenda.

The Constitution Act, 1982, is the most comprehensive use of constitutional arrangements to refashion the Canadian people that we have seen since Confederation. It emerged from a titanic intergovernmental struggle interspersed with bouts of manipulated populism. It contains within itself, as is noted below, the contradictions of the competing visions of the contestants who, except for the government of Quebec, were prepared to sign an agreement that none could wholeheartedly endorse. (The Meech Lake Accord, an even more recent attempt to remake community in Canada, is discussed in chapter 4.)

RECENT IMAGINED RECONSTRUCTIONS OF COMMUNITY

The road to the Constitution Act of 1982 is littered with competing visions of desired relations between communities and governments that fell by the wayside as the options narrowed. They are, however, not without interest, for they were all passionately espoused by influential actors at various times, and their defeat was not inevitable. Indeed, in the late 1970s the sovereignty-association option, or failing that the independence of Quebec, seemed not at all improbable as the allegiance of Québécois to Canada was underestimated. That the bout of constitutional introspection that produced the 1982 act ended with no improvement in regional representation at the centre was also an outcome that would not have been predicted by the constitutional intelligentsia of English Canada. On the contrary, had reform responded to the prevalent diagnosis and prescriptions in the anglophone political science community – that institutional reform must make the centre more representative of the regions – such a change would have been the first priority.

So, while our memories are still fresh, and before the victory of the Constitution Act is accorded an undeserved inevitability, it will be instructive to examine briefly a few of the unsuccessful reform proposals. They reveal by their diversity the profoundly varied and often contradictory constitutional relations between governments and societies that can be favourably envisaged by intelligent political élites once the sanctity of the existing order is challenged. Since these possibilities were not utopian dreams but realistic options, we must conclude that the existing societies and economies of the country could have adapted, under certain plausible conditions, to a rich variety of constitutional futures. Merely to cite such options is a salutary reminder, even if only speculative, of the modified civic identities and conceptions of community that we would have imbibed under the nurturance of differing arrangements. By implication, we are also reminded that who we are is a contingent achievement, the product of a particular history and geography and specific constitutional arrangements and policies – in brief, an ever-renewed evolutionary outcome that has no indefeasible entitlement to be the civic identity available for or chosen by our grandchildren.

We, and they, might have been shaped by the sovereignty-association option proposed by the Parti québécois, by various versions of federal-system renewal put forward under the capacious rubric of intrastate federalism, or by a renewed federalism transformed by the federally proposed Charter of Rights in association with Ottawa's preferred amending formula. None of this trilogy of possible constitutional futures, to be discussed below, was implemented, although a modified version of the federal Charter, coupled with the very different provincialist amending formula of the "Gang of Eight," is now part of the constitution. These three packages are far from exhausting the might-have-beens that surfaced in our long bout of constitutional introspection, but they will suffice for our objective of underlining the need to think of constitutional change as the master instrument of community transformation.

The PQ, Sovereignty-Association, and Canada without Quebec

The transformation sought by the Parti québécois (PQ) was based on the premise that the coexistence within the same constitutional order of the two ethnic nations of French and English, a minority and a majority respectively, was inherently damaging to the interests of the former. In the two distinct nations concealed "behind the fiction of ten provinces," in René Lévesque's phrase,[6] political power was driven by an ethnic dynamic. Thus English Canada naturally wields power on its own behalf in the central government and in the nine provincial governments where it is in the majority.[7] A litany of incidents, from Riel through conscription crises to assimilationist attitudes toward francophone minorities outside Quebec, provided much evidence for Lévesque's thesis. Further, Quebec, with the only government directly under majority francophone control, was constantly threatened, from the indépendantiste perspective, by the insatiable anglophone appetite for centralization. For the francophone majority in Quebec, this resulted in chronic insecurities and unstable, wavering identities hostile to the requirements for cultural growth in the contemporary world.

Throughout the PQ's nationalist advocacy runs the recurring image of a people who are not whole, who live "without an arm or a leg – or perhaps a heart."[8] There is also, as Handler points out, a negative vision, a pessimistic fear or recognition that survival is always precarious, always threatened. Thus language legislation is a response to "the cultural and linguistic disintegration of French-speaking Quebeckers," and a government role in cultural development is a response to "our state of advanced deculturalization."[9]

Independence-oriented Québécois nationalism is deeply hostile to the ambiguities inherent in federalism and thus resents Ottawa's natural tendency to foster a Canadian identity. The Québécois nation cannot survive in such a fluid environment in which its members are disoriented by the conflicting cues as to who they are that emanate from coexisting state authorities in Quebec City and in Ottawa. "The crucial axiom is always the same: an individual, human or collective, cannot be two things at once. To divide one's allegiance, affiliation, or identity is to court disaster."[10]

A vital national culture, according to PQ nationalist theory, requires a strong nurturing state with full jurisdictional capacity, "for coherent and efficient policy cannot be applied by a government if it has only partial powers and mere portions of the fiscal resources."[11] Such a state would have unimpeded access to its citizenry, unlike the Quebec government in Canadian federalism, whose system of dual loyalties "divides Quebeckers against themselves"[12] by generating a distracting allegiance to another government controlled by an ethnically and linguistically distinct majority. In McRoberts's summary, "the PQ coalition was united by the idea of the Quebec nation, and the necessity of its accession to independence."[13] To Lévesque, a cohesive society conscious of its identity that never experienced sovereignty would "always remain a tainted society."[14]

A separate, although related point, was that an independent Quebec would encounter less resistance to its nationalist purposes from anglophones and allophones within its borders when both of the latter were deprived of the emotional and practical support of Canadians outside Quebec, of the federal government, and of the Canadian constitution. One purpose of independence was to drive home to the English minority the message that Camille Laurin had delivered to them in 1978: "English-speakers had best learn to see themselves as a minority, not as the Quebec wing of the English-Canadian majority."[15] (Not surprising, the non-francophone minorities voted overwhelmingly against sovereignty-association in the 1980 referendum, recognizing that one of its purposes was to weaken their status, power, and recognition. The best estimates of the "yes" vote

among non-francophones "place it at no more than 5 per cent."[16])
Thus the independence movement sought constitutional change to
eliminate the direct influence over Québécois of Canadians outside
its borders wielding federal government powers and to strengthen
the political power of the province's French- speaking majority over
the internal minorities in its midst. Independence was to be a
straightforward instrument of nationalist affirmation for the francophone majority.

From the PQ's nationalist vantage point, federalism was thus clearly
both nation-dividing and -weakening, possibly even nation-
destroying. The thin layer of Canadianism fostered among Quebec's
francophones by the central government was nation-dividing, and
federalism's withholding of jurisdictional levers from Quebec's government was nation-weakening, because it inhibited the mobilization
required for successful nourishment of the small and beleaguered
French community in North America. As a province, stated Lévesque,
Quebec was only a "half-fledged state" whose government adminis-
tered a "truncated version of sovereignty."[17] In the summarizing
words of *Quebec-Canada: A New Deal*: "The fact that it is impossible,
in the present federal framework, for Québec to become a nation,
constitutes the very basis of the Canada-Québec political problem."[18]
The existing federal system could produce only a misshapen people.

While the political theory behind PQ nationalism logically led to
political independence, various practical and democratic considerations led to both the proposal for an economic association with Canada and the referendum by which sovereignty-association was to
achieve democratic legitimacy. The former was frequently described
as an appropriate recognition of economic interdependence that was
manifest internationally in the liberalized international trading order
generated by GATT. Also, of course, the idea of an economic association was designed to reassure a cautious electorate that change
would be orderly, as a high degree of continuity in economic relations
with Canada would accompany political severance. The latter, the
referendum, was intended to mobilize the community behind the PQ
project, to enhance Quebec's power at the bargaining table where
constitutional futures would be negotiated, and, presumably, to
ensure an auspicious base of community support for the future independent nation in a difficult transition period. Referenda, since more
than one might be required, were in themselves instruments to build
community consciousness in an era in which democratic consultations
were the most highly sanctioned bestowers of legitimacy. That the
referendum in fact gave resources to the Trudeau federalists was the

kind of unintended consequence that often attends high-risk strategies.

The unanswered community question that would have followed the complete independence of Quebec or negotiation of an economic association was the future of the left-over Canadians in the remaining nine provinces and two territories, suddenly possessed of a shrunken central government: a defeated majority whose pan-Canadian identity had been destroyed against its will.

In spite of the distinct possibility that the referendum might succeed in its mobilizing purposes and produce unpredictable consequences for the rest of Canada, there was negligible preparation for this state- and community-threatening danger. Not surprising, the manner in which Canada without Quebec would or should reconstitute itself was of little concern to Quebec's independence-seeking nationalist élite, as it introspectively focused on its own great history-making project. It was surprising, however, that the same absence of attention characterized governments and constitutional thinkers outside Quebec.

There were strategic reasons for this myopia: the desire not to give credibility to the possible division of Canada into two or more states, as well as the practical constraints that available resources had to be concentrated on keeping the country together. Nevertheless, the lack of preparation for the worst-case scenario, both within governments and among the public, would have been seriously debilitating in those confused early days when a Canada without Quebec would have begun to take shape or to disintegrate. The new definitions of community constructed by and for an English Canada unprepared to be on its own would have been profoundly affected by the shattered institutional legacy left by a departing Quebec.

At least initially, the breakup of Canada caused by Quebec independence would have been more damaging to the Canadianism than to the provincialism of the survivors. The defeated dream would have been the Canadian vision of a coast-to-coast country assiduously cultivated by the federal government, a country that had very recently come to acquire a self-definition as a bilingual people with two official languages. In marked contrast, however, to its devastating consequences for Canadianism, the triumph of Quebec nationalism could be viewed as a triumph of provincialism, admittedly carried to the extreme, that might have contagious effects on the incumbent political élites in the capitals of the other nine provinces. In general, their reaction through the 1970s to Quebec's challenge to the country's survival had been to see it as an opportunity to gain advantages for their own provincial governments and peoples. Thus, given the contrast between surviving and powerful provincial élites and a defeated and reduced Canadian élite deprived of its historic raison d'être, at least the early attempts of constitution-making for a Canada without Quebec would have been responsive to a centrifugal provincialism of governments.

The difficulty that Canada without Quebec would have had in coming to grips with its new and unsought existence would have been – until the dust had cleared – a repeat of the difficulty experienced by English Canada throughout the constitutional debates. The PQ's effort to portray Canada as composed of two nations, with Quebec's government speaking for one of them, fell on deaf ears in English Canada, simply because English Canada has no corporate existence. It lacks a government of its own that it can employ as an instrument of its political desires. The provincial governments outside Quebec speak only for the provincial dimension of English-Canadian existence.

Such an aggregation of provincialisms does not constitute a political voice for English Canada as the majority nation in the two-nation definition of Canada hypothesized by some Quebec nationalists. Further, the central government, especially in its recent dualist phase, can be viewed as the government of English Canada only by partisans whose ideology blinds their vision. In the more than four decades since Louis St Laurent assumed office in 1948, the prime ministership has been held by Quebecers for more than thirty years. Regardless, however, of who is prime minister, Ottawa cannot be other than the government of all Canadians, incorporating and expressing all the major cleavages to which Canada is subject. The Report of the Task Force on Canadian Unity (1979) lucidly expresses the dualistic imperative that informs that viewpoint: "Canada, seen from the federal government's perspective, is a linguistically dual federal state composed of two societies – one French-speaking and one English-speaking – which extend geographically beyond the borders of any one province. Thus the federal government believes that it is necessary that this linguistic duality be more fully reflected in Canada's central political institutions and in federal policies and programs."[19]

These observations suggest the following three summary points about the relation of anglophone Canada to the constitution:

1 - The constitution does not provide anglophone Canadians with any political outlet or government authority through which they can speak as such.

2 - The political voice of anglophone Canada is either fragmented into provincial arenas or is, and must be, combined with the other

linguistic national community in the operations of the federal government.

3 - These constitutional considerations make it extremely difficult for anglophone Canada even to conceive of itself as an actual or potential political community and thus to make plans for an independent future without Quebec. The existing federal system, especially when Ottawa is sensitive to Canada's historic French-English duality, pulls anglophone Canada away from a sense of itself. It either reduces it to competing provincialisms or incorporates it into a dualistic pan-Canadianism.

Ultimately, these structural considerations explain why no one spoke for English Canada in the constitutional debates. No government could undertake the task, and a spokesperson lacking government connections would have been rootless and devoid of the legitimacy conferred by possession of political office.

Intrastate Federalism

The sovereignty-association analysis defined the constitutional problem as the conflicting coexistence of two nations, the contemporary version of the French and English "founding peoples," in a system that could not satisfy the aspirations of both peoples simultaneously. The logical power of that two-nations analysis required retreat of the French fact to Quebec, treatment of Canada outside Quebec as English-Canadian territory, and consequently relative indifference to francophone minorities in English Canada and to non-francophone minorities – anglophone and allophone – in Quebec.

The intrastate federalism debate, by contrast, defined the Canadian problem as the need to find new institutional/constitutional arrangements to express better the provincial dimension within the structures and functioning of the federal government. The tendencies to equate federalism with the division of powers and to assume that the provincial aspect of Canadians' existence could be adequately channeled through provincial governments were both challenged by the intrastate analysis.

The terminology of intrastate federalism was received in the 1970s as an innovative contribution to the lens through which both scholars and practitioners viewed federalism. Nevertheless, there is a sense in which it was simply a restatement of a perennial issue in federal systems – in the Canadian case, how either the provincial or national dimension of our existence should influence the exercise of government power at the other level, or what the mechanisms should be for what J.R. Mallory called "the interpenetration of one level of govern-

ment by the other."[20] K.C. Wheare, the distinguished British constitutional scholar, described the arrangements of 1867 as quasi-federal
precisely because of the many instruments available to the national
government to intervene in provincial arenas.[21] These included dis-
allowance and declaratory powers, appointment of the lieutenant-
governor, the latter's discretionary power to reserve provincial legislation, and federal appointment of superior, district, and county court
judges.

The term *intrastate federalism*, coined by Donald Smiley in 1971,
turned Wheare's quasi-federalism upside down with its suggestion
that a constitutional response to aggressive provincialism need not
take the form of decentralization via the division of powers. Refashioning of the central government to make it more responsive to provincial concerns could perhaps challenge the "alarming extent [to
which] Canadian interests and attitudes which are territorially delim-
ited have come to find an outlet exclusively through the provincial
governments."[22]

This intrastate analysis became virtually a new conventional wisdom
in the 1970s, especially among political scientists. Its positive reception
was facilitated by the regional imbalance in the Trudeau-led Liberal
party, which governed with only one brief interruption from 1968 to
1984 and which, except after its first election victory, in 1968, had
limited representation in its caucus from the three prairie provinces
and only a bit more from British Columbia. Quebec's virtual exclusion
from the Conservative caucus during Joe Clark's short-lived Conservative interlude (1979–80) provided additional confirmation that
single-party government often experienced serious deficiencies of
regional representation on the government side of the House.

Its intellectual and political profile was greatly enhanced in the
mid- to late 1970s when the governments of the four western provinces entered the constitutional debate in a serious way. The Social
Credit government of British Columbia, in particular, became a powerful advocate of intrastate reforms that would increase its influence
as a government in national politics, mainly by the vehicle of a
reformed Senate dominated by provincial governments.

The basic intrastate thesis, which surfaced in numerous proposals
for constitutional reform, was that Ottawa, constrained by the British
practice of responsible parliamentary government and its concomitant of party discipline, was insensitive to the pervasive regionalism
and dualism which the Pepin-Robarts Report (1979) saw as the defining characteristics of Canadian society. In practical terms, as that
report indicated, existing arrangements facilitated the harnessing of
dualism and regionalism by provincial governments and thus trans-

lated those powerful social forces into agents of provincialism. Regionalism slid into provincialism because no other conceptions of regionalism had the governmental power equivalent to that of a province behind them. The francophone side of dualism was translated into a threatening provincialism by the drive of Quebec's government to become the sole legitimate representative of a French Canada restricted to Quebec, and redefined as Québécois. For well-known reasons, the Senate, the obvious instrument for injecting the provincial dimension into the federal government, had only limited capacity as a believable advocate of provincial/regional concerns.

Given the hypothesized inability of the federal government effectively to incorporate and represent the primary sociological realities of Canada, labelled territorial particularisms by Smiley, that government was considered to be rootless. Accordingly, the provinces were viewed as having more legitimacy than jurisdiction, and the federal government as having more jurisdiction than legitimacy.

Since the intrastate perspective was hostile to restoring equilibrium by transferring jurisdiction to the provinces, the logical solution was to enhance Ottawa's legitimacy. Since the latter's attenuated legitimacy was attributed to its inadequate contact and empathy with provincial values and concerns, the solution was to incorporate provincial perspectives into its workings, a process often described as federalizing central-government institutions, or rather more bluntly by the Canada West Foundation as injecting "greater regional political muscle into decision-making at the federal government level."[23]

The governing assumption, in Smiley's language, was that "territorialism is the dominant circumstance of our political life. The institutional imperative then is to so modify our political structures as to secure the more effective channelling of territorially-demarcated attitudes and interests through the central government rather than the provinces alone."[24] The institutions through which this goal was to be achieved were as varied as the ingenuity of reformers and included the Supreme Court, both houses of Parliament, the bureaucracy, and federal boards and agencies.

It soon became evident, however, that the evocative phrase "federalizing central government institutions" had two quite different meanings that were not always adequately distinguished in the early days of the debate. One meaning, provincialist intrastate reform, usually involved a revamped Senate whose members were to be appointed by and accountable to provincial governments and that would have responsibilities for monitoring and if necessary vetoing federal programs, policies, and appointments considered to be especially salient for provincial governments and their communities.[25]

Such reformers wished to bring provincial governments directly, if selectively, into the workings of the central government. Their proposals tended to accord minimal significance to the Senate's traditional second-chamber role of reviewing and revising legislation received from the Commons and to stress a new role of managing – in ways that were not always clear – the interdependence of governments in the federal system.

The second meaning, centralist intrastate reform, typically involved restructuring of representation in such federal institutions as the bureaucracy, the House of Commons (by electoral reform), the Senate, and various boards and agencies. The major purpose was to enhance Ottawa's provincial sensitivity in ways that did not involve provincial governments or their delegates intruding in national affairs, especially in Parliament. The clear objective was to weaken the capacity of provincial governments to assume a roving mandate on the national stage on behalf of allegedly provincial interests, regardless of jurisdictional niceties, by allowing Ottawa more effectively to represent provincial concerns. The incorporation of provincialism directly into the centre would facilitate provincialism's blending with the pan-Canadian vision appropriate to the federal government. The assumption was that strengthening Ottawa's provincial credentials would reduce provincial governments' propensity to speak for provincial values and interests in matters under federal jurisdiction.

As Richard Vernon suggestively observes, a federation is not merely a regime of co-ordinate governing authorities but also postulates and generates co-ordinate citizenship. To divide authority, in other words, is also to divide the citizen. In a system of classical federalism, in which both orders of government scrupulously respect their jurisdictional boundaries, the federal citizen's task of dividing his/her identities and loyalties is relatively straightforward.[26] However, as Vernon notes, citizenship is immensely more complicated in intrastate versions of federalism, where the national dimension of politics also incorporates the provincial orientations of the citizenry.

Precisely how versions of intrastate federalism might reshape the dual citizen identities, loyalties, and sense of belonging of a federal people is not easily answered. It would depend partly on constitutional particulars, whose societal consequences are beyond the limited predictive capacities of contemporary social science. The few following, crude paragraphs, therefore, can remind us that constitutional reform changes simultaneously civic identities and the nature of citizenship, even if there is limited agreement on the precise nature of that change.

Both centralist and provincialist intrastate perspectives would have brought provincial and national identities and loyalties into more intimate contact in the psyches of individuals, for their very purpose was to bring a provincial dimension to the policy discussion of matters under national jurisdiction. Conceivably, depending on the nature and extent of intrastate reforms, the citizen might rarely see purely national actors taking decisive action in response to their own independent assessments of the needs and interests of the single pan-Canadian community. As Jennifer Smith cogently observes, proposals for intrastate federalism are based on the thesis that the separation of local and national issues is impossible and that a distinctive "national political discourse liberated from local concerns" is not tenable, thus denying key assumptions on which the original Confederation agreement was based.[27]

Nevertheless, within the common features discerned by Smith, it is obvious that the superficially similar perspectives of centralist v. provincialist versions of intrastate reform in fact postulated very different shaping purposes to the constitutional/institutional changes they sought. The provincialist model sought not only to enhance the significance of provincial communities relative to the national community but to do so by extending the capacity of provincial governments to represent, and thus to shape, the communities they governed, with respect to matters hitherto thought of as subject to federal jurisdiction. The dual civic identity of the citizens of a federal state would be readjusted to strengthen provincial identities relative to a pan-Canadian one, to weaken an autonomous national identity, to reflect a fusion of their provincial and country-wide selves in the national arena, and to link the identities and perceptions of provincial residents more tightly to the cues transmitted by the now more powerful incumbent provincial government élites. This system, designed to extend the sphere within which provincial governments could speak authoritatively for their people, was necessarily hostile to the expression of intraprovincial diversities in central government settings. There was little agreement on whether giving such provincial representatives a national platform would moderate their provincialism, as Pepin-Robarts believed, or simply legitimate the frustration of federal initiatives by untamed provincial plenipotentiaries, as some critics feared.

The centralist intrastate version, by contrast, typically sought the input of a moderate provincialism, detached from provincial governments, that was to be incorporated in a subordinate way into the country-wide vision of a Canadian people that was more than an aggregation of their provincial selves. Diverse, even contradictory, viewpoints from individual provinces were not deplored. Some federal proposals gave them exaggerated representation, as in Bill c-6o's proposals for Senate reform, the better to confirm that no provincial government spoke for a monolithic citizenry – that its voice, indeed, was only one of many provincial voices.[28] From the citizens' perspective, his/her provincial identity would have diffuse, fragmented representation on the national stage. It would accordingly be less resistant to assimilation in a pan-Canadian national orientation than would be citizens represented by provincial government–appointed élites in a reformed Senate dominated by the provinces. In addition, of course, unlike reforms suggested by provincial governments in the 1970s, Ottawa's proposals were always sensitive to one of the upper house's traditional roles, as a chamber of sober second thought – a responsibility that would have de-emphasized the provincial orientations of new senators and thus of the residents of the provinces for whom they spoke.

In both versions of intrastate reform, however, the provincial/regional dimension would have been given added weight in the governing of Canada. Conversely, especially in the provincialist version, the flow of national influence into matters under provincial jurisdiction would be filtered, checked, and attenuated.

The intrastate perspective structured the reform agenda around the representation of regionalism, immediately redefined as provincialism. The intrastate debate was a debate about federalism which attributed Ottawa's weakness and the strength of the provinces to the latters' much greater access to the sources of governmental vitality and legitimacy – provincial identities and communities. Ottawa's weakness reflected the weakness of the national community on which it rested. Only by becoming more provincial could the national government be strengthened.

To accept these terms for the constitutional debate normally worked against any conception of a Canadian community composed of individual rights-bearing citizens. Accordingly, the intrastate perspective tended to be unsympathetic to the political philosophy of a charter and hostile to political perceptions of the Canadian community that stressed sex, ethnic, cultural, racial, linguistic, aboriginal, life-style and other cleavages that were not demarcated by provincial boundaries. Although some reform proposals, such as those of Pepin-Robarts, overcame this bias and recommended both intrastate federalism and a charter, more purist intrastate perspectives naturally found their most ardent advocates among provincial governments. The federal government displayed only spasmodic interest, almost invariably opted for the centralist variant which did not enhance provincial governments' power, and was always apprehensive that the too explicit recognition of regionalism at the centre would foster it at the expense of a national community which, federal officials reiterated, was more than an aggregation of provincial communities.

Neither version of the intrastate reform thrust, which generated dozens of supportive proposals from governments, professional associations, and individuals found its way into the revised 1982 constitution.

The Federal Amending Formula and the Charter

Shortly after the breakdown of the First Ministers' Conference in September 1980, Prime Minister Trudeau announced that the federal government would proceed, unilaterally if necessary, to request the United Kingdom's Parliament to amend the BNA Act one last time. The limited proposals to be sent to Westminster – a Charter of Rights binding on both orders of government, a complicated process for determining within Canada a domestic amending formula within a limited time period,[29] and patriation as a by-product of the latter – threatened major surgery on Canadian federalism. As the proposals were modified in the parliamentary committee hearings, that threat was strengthened.

The federal package is not the relatively unmodified source of the Constitution Act of 1982: the amending formula that Ottawa proposed for consideration after patriation was pre-empted by intergovernmental agreement, excluding Quebec, on an alternative formula. Its significance lies rather in the overall coherence of its guiding assumptions. This coherence – the package's components were shaped by the guiding vision of a single government and thus unsullied by the compromises of executive federalism – contrasted dramatically with the lack of symmetry, discussed below, in the actual Constitution Act that Canadians received in 1982.

The most important component of the federal package was the Charter of Rights. Trudeau put the Charter at the top of the agenda as soon as he realized that constitutional discussions were unavoidable. He sought to "entrench the shared political values of all Canadians in constitutional law."[30] The Charter was always more than an instrument to protect the rights of Canadians against their governments. The larger political purpose, which explains its tenacious sponsorship by the federal government, was to strengthen national unity by providing constitutional support to a new definition of Canadians as a rights-bearing citizenry regardless of location.[31] These rights, enforceable against both orders of government, were intended to strengthen the Canadian component of civic identity by being uniformly available and by limiting the capacity of federalism to generate diverse treatment of citizens as demarcated by provincial boundaries. As it emerged from the Special Joint Committee of the Senate and of the House of Commons on the Constitution, the Charter also contained clauses of special interest to women, aboriginals, multicultural Canadians, the disabled, and others who were thus promised constitutional identities and status they had previously lacked. Their recognition was at least a weak dissent from the proposition that the only really important communities were those directly linked, as national and provincial communities, to the governments of Canadian federalism.

A central objective of the Charter, directly responsible for section 23 dealing with minority-language educational rights, was to provide constitutional support, subject to certain explicit conditions being met, for the provision of French-language education for francophones outside Quebec, and English-language education for anglophones inside the province. These provisions were designed to counter Quebec nationalists' tendency to equate French Canada with Quebec by strengthening simultaneously the anglophone minority within the province and the francophone minorities elsewhere.[32] To keep alive by constitutional means a non-francophone minority within Quebec would render illegitimate the claim of Quebec's government to speak for an ethnic nation and thus would continually remind the nationalist élite of the ambiguities in the concept of Québécois. The survival of francophone minorities elsewhere would counter the linked nationalist claims that only in Quebec could the French language thrive and that only its government could be trusted to be its defender. The constitutional obligation on the provinces of English Canada to provide education in the French language would bluntly remind them of their national responsibilities.

From the constitutional theory perspective, the Charter generated a traditional debate over parliamentary supremacy versus support for judicial leadership in the protection of entrenched rights. The real debate, however, was about community – should the constitution foster a coast-to-coast community of Canadians whose rights were to be protected against both orders of government? Such protection would constrain the range of policy choices available to provincial governments by setting a floor of Charter-defined Canadianism which they could not violate. Consequently, provincial governments in a post-Charter era would have not only to pursue their province-building goals within the framework of the division of powers but to do so with respect to a minimum floor of rights. In practical terms, a powerful dimension of Canadianism, defined by rights, would become a ubiquitous provincial presence, monitoring the exercise of otherwise legitimate provincial jurisdictional powers. Such a Charter would also logically induce provincial residents to view and judge their governments through the standardized lens of Canadian citizenship rather than the more variable lens of provincial residence.

It is entirely understandable, given these considerations, that the prospect of a Canada-wide entrenched Charter binding on both orders of government was not viewed with similar enthusiasm by central- and provincial-government élites. For the former, such a Charter has the positive effect that it generates a limited definition of a national community which constrains both orders of government. A national community is not restricted to "section-91 Canada" (as defined in the BNA Act) but in a different version, and via a Charter, is given expression in provincial arenas as well. The absence of this latter feature in the Canadian Bill of Rights, 1960, which did not extend to provincial jurisdiction because Prime Minister Diefenbaker anticipated opposition from provincial governments, was frequently identified as one of its major shortcomings. Nevertheless, Diefenbaker's underlying philosophy, as well as that of other supporters of a Bill of Rights in the 1940s and 1950s, was hostile to provincial variations in rights. To have "fundamental human rights ... dependent upon one's provincial address," he asserted in 1952, "would [produce] ... a Balkanized Canada."[33]

Although Diefenbaker and Trudeau were intent on containing different centrifugal forces by the instrument of rights, similarities in their pan-Canadianism deserve an extended exploration at which I can only hint. The continuity between the criticisms of the provincial balkanization of rights by early rights supporters in the 1940s and 1950s, and similar arguments by Trudeau and others in their later Charter advocacy, powerfully confirms the association of rights with the idea of the nation-state. There is an imperialist aspect to the concept of rights that resists its application only to the national jurisdiction in federal systems. The overwhelming response to the varied weaknesses of Diefenbaker's Bill of Rights, including its non-application to the provinces, was not to give up the idea of a Bill of Rights as an experiment that had failed but to produce a stronger bill, entrench it, and extend it to provincial jurisdiction. Equally revealing, if my impressions are correct, the Charter's section 33 override power – which enables a government to sustain legislation, for renewable five-year periods, in conflict with section 2 or sections 7 to 15 of the Charter – is on the defensive. At least in English Canada, rights consciousness generates a culture that is hostile to exceptions, to variations, and in general to differential availability of rights. Such variation appears to offend against the universalism inherent in the idea of a rights-bearing citizenry.

The idea of entrenched rights binding on both orders of government was much less attractive to provincial political élites. By the late 1970s, opposition to constitutionally entrenched rights constraining both orders was centred in provincial governments. The federal government's much greater international involvement, including its prominent UN participation, made it much more susceptible to the international forces behind the global rights revolution. More important, it viewed favourably the nation-building purposes served by rights. Provincial governments' opposition flowed equally naturally from their structural location in the federal system. Since the justification of their existence resides in provincially bounded territorial diversity, they have little incentive to look favourably on instruments designed to constrain that very diversity.

Thus, although provincial opponents spoke the British language of parliamentary supremacy, their purpose was preservation of provincial autonomy on behalf of the federalist values of regional diversity. The critics, especially Allan Blakeney, Sterling Lyon, and René Lévesque, clearly understood the practical constraints on provincial autonomy that a Charter could bring and, equally important, the pan-Canadian symbolism of rights that it would spread through their provincial electorates.

The Charter's nation-building purposes were reinforced by a proposed amending formula that displayed perhaps the most explicitly dismissive attitude to the provinces of any federal government since Confederation.[34] The formula weakened the provincial governments' role in the amending process, elevated the constitutional status of the citizenry with its referendum provisions, and facilitated the overriding of provincial objections by specially constructed national majorities. Based on a four-region Canada – Ontario, Quebec, the Atlantic provinces, and the west – the formula required the support of the legislative assemblies of Quebec and Ontario, of any two western and any two Atlantic provinces, and of the federal parliament for the passage of an amendment.[35] Since the opposition of up to four provinces could not hold up an amendment, the formula was clearly disrespectful of provincial sovereignty. Its relative flexibility was tied to the federal government's objective of strengthening the capacity of a national will to get its way against the selective opposition of at least several of the less powerful provincial governments.

Its constitutional radicalism, however, was evidenced less by its regional requirements for approval – modelled closely on the Victoria

Charter, which had just fallen short of intergovernmental agreement in 1971 – than on a supplementary amending provision. In the absence of agreement by provincial legislatures, Ottawa could call a national referendum; a proposed amendment could be passed by a national voting majority accompanied by a majority in those provinces the support of whose legislatures would have constituted provincial approval of the proposed amendment. Theoretically, an amendment could be passed even if opposed by referendum voting majorities in four provinces equally distributed in the west and in Atlantic Canada and also opposed by all ten provincial governments.[36]

The formula was a major rearrangement, both symbolic and practical, of the relative status of key actors in the constitutional system. Sovereignty was awarded to an alliance between a Canadian referendum electorate and the federal government, with the former voting on constitutional proposals that might have been drafted by federal officials to serve federal interests. The clear purpose of the formula was to enhance the constitutional leverage of Ottawa, transform citizens into significant but still dependent constitutional actors, weaken their ties with provincial governments, and remove the capacity of the latter, via their legislative assemblies, to speak definitively for provincial interests in constitutional amendment processes. The referendums, by which the latter reduction of provincial governments' status and power was to be achieved, "are devices not only to give voice to popular sentiments but also to create and recreate a political community by the symbolism attached to participation in a dramatic political act. In the last analysis, the strengthening of community by governments is a way of strengthening the governments which claim to speak for them."[37]

In the new constitutional regime, provincial powers would be conditional rather than secure. The federal government clearly and properly assumed that provincial electorates, perhaps especially when addressed in their national capacity, would be less rigid defenders of provincial interests than provincial governments would be. By contrast, the federal government, possessed of its own veto and the exclusive power to initiate referendums, could not lose.

Of course, had such an amending procedure been instituted, its use might have been rare, and the performance of future referendum electorates might have belied the centralists' aspirations. In Australia, as Russell notes, the electorate has not been sympathetic to constitutional proposals to enhance the powers of the Commonwealth government.[38] Even so, the theory and symbolism of the constitution would have been permanently altered. An amending formula answers the supreme constitutional question of where sovereignty lies. Compared to prior practice and to the major contending proposals, the answer provided by this formula was a repudiation of provincial governments.

By means of the amending formula and the Charter, the Trudeau-led federal government sought to transform the Canadian political system by reshuffling relations between governments and peoples. As McRoberts correctly observes: "For Trudeau and for many of his colleagues, the primary purpose of political life always had been to implant a new conception of the Canadian political community and of the role the federal government should play as a 'national government,' the government of all Canadians."[39] Accordingly, Ottawa's constitutional response to the centrifugal forces it feared could break up the country was not to accommodate them. Rather, it fought back, on the premise that provincial governments were far more weakly rooted than the strident provincialism of the premiers suggested and that a coast-to-coast nation was struggling to find a constitutional expression that Ottawa was more than willing to provide.

The federal government disagreed with the basic intrastate assumption of deep-seated provincialism that could be accommodated only by making new outlets for its expression within national institutions. The basic federal hypothesis was that the existing power and status accorded to provincial governments thwarted and fragmented a Canadian nationalism that would flourish under a different constitutional regime. With its symbiotic package of a nationalizing Charter and an amending formula that allowed appeal to a specially constructed national majority of citizens, Ottawa hoped to move closer to that different and better constitutional arrangement.

For the Parti québecois (PQ), the pan-Canadian community sustained by the existing constitution and by the federal government's policies was, at least for Québécois, an artificial community that, nevertheless, inhibited the creative flowering of the Québécois culture and identity that would emerge under Quebec sovereignty. The federal government believed the reverse, that the Canadian community was deeply rooted and potentially vibrant but that it lacked appropriate institutional outlets for its expression. Thus both the PQ and the governing federal Liberals believed that the existing structure of Canadian federalism frustrated creative maturation of the community of concern to them. Although they disagreed on the nature of the existing system's bias and on the identity of the community that was repressed, they both sought to strengthen their community by removing impediments to, and creating more channels for, its self-expression.

CONSTITUTIONAL CHANGE
AND THE TRANSFORMATION
OF COMMUNITY

The above commentaries on proposals for and experiments in the constitutional refashioning of community can be distilled into certain elementary conclusions.[40]

1 - Most community-oriented constitutional change is future directed, designed to pull a people in new directions, or to erect bulwarks against unwanted change. It has vanguard, élitist attributes. It is not helpful, therefore, to assess constitutional proposals just in terms of their fit with prevailing realities, except in the sense of the latter as a point of departure. If there is no discrepancy between what is, or what will otherwise be, and the future condition toward which constitutional change is directed, then such change should be characterized as window dressing.

2 - Canadian politicians clearly understand that community is not a given, but a creation. They recognize that the federal system exists as an appropriate response to the coexistence of the national and provincial communities on which it rests. They also recognize, however, that, as both orders of government intervene in their societies and economies, they continuously recreate, by their policies and incentives, the communities they serve. Contemporary Canadian citizens are still being drawn into provincial or national networks of policy and administration by old and new government programs shaped by a nineteenth-century division of powers. To shape community by constitutional restructuring is merely to continue the daily routine of government in a more exalted atmosphere where the stakes are higher. Governments realize, accordingly, that the relative salience to the citizenry of the national and provincial communities waxes and wanes partly in accordance with what governments do, which in turn is influenced by the instruments at their disposal, which can be modified by constitutional change.

3 - Canadian society is criss-crossed by multiple cleavages. Proposals for constitutional reform normally attempt to enhance or depress particular cleavages. Those who govern consider cleavages to be determined not exclusively by socioeconomic forces but also by the latter's interaction with political and constitutional factors. Accordingly, governments seek to support cleavages most compatible with their own interests. Advocates of intrastate federalism, particularly of the provincialist variety, sought to enhance the significance of province/region and weaken the power of the national community and of national majorities based on the arithmetic equality of all

citizens. Sovereignty-association conceived of Canada in terms of two nations and was thus hostile to cross-cutting political cleavages which, by stressing interdependence and mutuality of interest with Canadians elsewhere, undermined exclusive identification with Quebec. Breaking out of federalism was a way of reducing cross-cutting cleavages. The federal Liberals, by contrast, sought to play down French Canada's identification with Quebec by policy designed to keep alive the substance and symbol of a country-wide Canada in which the French language could flourish outside Quebec. Federal proposals typically played down the importance of provincial borders, stressed the heterogeneity within provinces, and sought to strengthen cleavages indifferent to provincial location.

4 - Federalism involves the coexistence of two orders of government with separate jurisdictional responsibilities which govern a common citizenry. Both the federal and provincial governments are concerned that the policies of the "other" will conflict with their own policies and/or will subject members of "their" community to contradictory requirements. One way to overcome this is by intergovernmental co-operation and practices of shared rule. Another strategy, and one of the basic purposes of constitutional change, is to design instruments to make the "other" order of government conscious of and sensitive to the other's concerns. Thus, for the federal government, one crucial purpose of the Charter was to make provincial governments respectful of and responsive to a set of Canadian values entrenched as Charter rights. Conversely, advocates of intrastate constitutional reform all sought to bring a stronger provincial dimension to bear in Ottawa's political processes. Provincial governments sought to increase the presence and impact of provincial values in the federal government; and the latter sought to increase the presence and impact of Canadian values in provincial arenas.

5 - Constitutional change aimed at transforming community rests on some theory of how society works. If the theory is wrong, the change is unlikely to have the desired effect. Thus Banting and Simeon correctly note that many of the predictions about the likely effect of a Charter of Rights are tenuous at best, because of the difficulty of "link[ing] institutions and behaviour, especially when the full consequences of some changes may not develop for a long period."[41] Once a constitutional change is effected, the new system will be worked by private actors bringing the infinitely varied interests of a free society to their calculations.

6 - Elite-held theories of constitutional change are much influenced by the instruments available for their implementation. The question

"What is to be done?" always has to be put into the context of a particular set of resources and the existing constraints on and opportunities for action. Politicians, accordingly, seek to increase their power and freedom of manoeuvre in the process of constitutional change and/or to restrict those of their opponents. Thus, for the PQ the 1980 referendum was not only a response to democratic values but also an attempt to enhance the Quebec government's bargaining power at the post-referendum conference table. From the time of the PQ victory in 1976, the federal government sought to weaken the thesis that unanimity was necessary before major constitutional change could be requested from the United Kingdom's parliament. From Ottawa's perspective, unanimity gave a change-blocking veto to the government least likely to be sympathetic to the direction of change the federal government expected to pursue. As noted above, the federal government proposed an amending formula that was designed to increase its own manoeuvrability and to weaken the blocking capacities of the provincial governments.

POINTS 5 AND 6 UNDERLINE the very practical nature of the theory of constitutional change held by those who try to engineer it, the intermingling of means and ends involved in its pursuit, the impediments that stand in the way of a single government's scoring a decisive triumph in the face of rival governments with competing objectives, and the probability that the final product will contain enough imperfections to disgust the purist.

The seriousness of these imperfections may not be immediately apparent to those who fashion the compromise that contains them. That discovery may be left to the successor generation, which, in working the recently modified arrangements, brings to the surface practical contradictions that were not anticipated, or were thought of as only verbal, or academic, by their original creators. As the next two chapters indicate, that appears to be the case with the Constitution Act of 1982. We can now see, from the vantage point of the Meech Lake package, that the 1982 compromise is Janus-faced on the central issue of sovereignty, vacillating between awarding it to governments via the amending formula and somewhat less directly to citizens by the rights that the Charter accords them.

CONCLUSION

A people is constantly redefining its collective sense of itself – coming to terms with changing ethnic and linguistic composition and the infinitely varied heterogeneity that modern conditions generate. And it does so in a global environment that unceasingly generates new criteria by which peoplehood is to be judged.

For a federal people, the task has special complexities not present in a unitary state. Whatever the founding document states about the relative powers of the two orders of government – and thus about the anticipated future importance of the country-wide and provincial communities they serve – the founding is best seen not as providing a rigid code of final answers but as a point of departure in an unending journey in which the constitution is continuously remade, sometimes self-consciously, and sometimes by the cumulative effect of random events and of policies and decisions directed to areas other than the constitution.

The continuous remaking of our federal and provincial selves as we work the living constitution of Canadian federalism, however, now encompasses a diminishing proportion of the task of constitutional self-definition in which we are engaged. Federalism no longer exhausts our identities, and the constitutional significance of the historic priority of French and English as founding peoples is now on the defensive. Our linguistic duality is now thoroughly impregnated with the ethnic and racial diversities of a people who are decreasingly British and French by background. Status Indians are no longer isolated, voteless, and voiceless, The emergence of a new constitutional category "aboriginal" in section 35 of the Constitution Act, 1982, defined as including the Indian, Inuit, and Métis peoples of Canada, gives official encouragement to an enlargement of the indigenous population of Canada, while adding to that population's internal complexity. From now on, the constitution's link with ethnicity must go beyond French-English duality.

Bemused as we sometimes are by the fixity of labels such as "nation," we may underestimate the adaptation that is required if our continuity as a people is not to falter. In fact, Canadians have experienced a remarkable transformation of their collective identities since the Second World War. That change has been most evident in Quebec and in the pan-Canadian dimension of our existence. To compare the Tremblay Report's description of Quebec society in the mid 1950s[42] with the society to be served by independence, as described in the referendum paper *Quebec-Canada: A New Deal*,[43] is to be struck by the different worlds that the two documents inhabit. And, not surprising, the constitutional options espoused by these two Québécois public introspections are profoundly influenced by their different views of the people they have become and aspire to be.

One is no less struck by a contrast in collective self-definitions of the Canadian identity in the era of King and Drew with what we have inherited after four decades of change. To move from the former to the latter is to observe striking decline in the British contribution to the Canadian self-image and marked diffusion of a rights consciousness. In the case of neither Quebec nor of Canada writ large did this evolution just happen. Although change was partly driven from below, it was also partly orchestrated and managed from above by political élites.

Not all these changes in how Canadians see themselves were results of explicit constitutional change, narrowly conceived as restricted to formal amendments. Policies related to language and culture, along with others directed to such symbols of our existence as flags, anthems, and the ethnic background and sex of our governors-general and lieutenant-governors, were in essence constitutional. They were, in each case, state-sponsored cues to remind us that our little Canadian world had changed and that we must, in the public interest, change the criteria by which we define and evaluate each other.

This nurturing of an image is occasionally denigrated as "only symbolic" by those who do not understand how societies function and who know little of Canadian history. Those issues that have most deeply divided us, and have agitated our passions to the point of frenzy, have revolved around race, ethnicity, religion, and language, all of which have pervasive symbolic overtones. The very citizenship that unites a people by bridging such divisions, and the patriotism that induces heroism and self-sacrifice, are themselves symbols, contributions to a symbolic and normative order that restrains centrifugal forces.

The task of holding a society together has not eased in modern conditions. The multiplication of cleavages that attends the high degree of self-consciousness of our era, and the fragmentation that derives from the multiple pasts in the memories of a multicultural and multiracial society, require transcending if we are to make our coexistence meaningful and fruitful. Since 1945 we have had one of the most rapidly growing electorates in the Western world. Each addition to our numbers from outside Canada diminishes the capacity of a common past to unite us. As between French and English, that common past has never existed in the socialization experiences of the young. Even in Quebec, however, as language policies recruit newcomers to the francophone community, references to the Conquest of 1759–60 decreasingly tap a shared memory. And, as Paquet observes, "Dans un monde d'identités multiples et contrastées, d'i-dentités en formation et en décomposition, il est improbable que cette 'mutualité' naisse organiquement."[44] In Quebec, as in Canada, the community must be defined in civic terms, applicable to all, if it is not to be an instrument of exclusion.[45] Those definitions require resort to instruments and policies of province-building and nation-building for which charters and bills of rights are prominent candidates.

I would go further; it is difficult to believe that our small population in possession of the second largest country in the world can move in any direction other than becoming more multiracial and multicultural. Impoverished, persecuted humanity elsewhere will not leave us alone. And we already are so ethnically plural that to close the doors now offends citizen compatriots who are already here. Canadians, through their governments, have been responding to Rousseau's question from *The Social Contract*: "How can a man or a people seize an immense territory and keep it from the rest of the world except by a punishable usurpation, since all others are being robbed by such an act, of the places of habitation and the means of subsistence which nature gave them in common?"[46]

The normative message behind Rousseau's observation explains why the modern democratic state, especially if it has large land borders, can no longer control the movement of people across its own frontiers. "Affluent and free countries," notes Michael Walzer, "are like élite universities; they are besieged by applicants."[47] Where the legalities are intimidating and frontiers are permeable, illegal access increases. Underground populations of illegal migrants are the human counterpart of the underground economy; in fact, the two are often interrelated attempts to escape the reach of the state. Some estimates suggest that there may be between 3.5 and 5.5 million undocumented migrants living and working in the United States.[48] Canada, too, has many such migrants, though proportionately fewer than its southern neighbour.

If this then is our future, the Charter of Rights appears not just as one answer to our recent constitutional troubles but also as an anticipatory response to future diversities. Most modern nations are in effect empires governing many tribes and peoples. They cannot leave the practice of community and the understanding of rights to customs and traditions that are shared by shrinking proportions of the population and that presupposed a more homogeneous society.[49]

We cannot, of course, be saved by charters and constitutions alone, but the latter have a key role to play in what Gilles Paquet, following Tussman, describes as "shaping the institutions of awareness."[50]

Across the great divides of provinces and ethnicity, perhaps the most essential vehicle to bring us together is a strengthened sense of citizenship that cannot be left to the free play of forces in the social market but requires nurturing by the state. In that educational task, and admitting all of its weaknesses, the Charter is a central weapon. Thus, future historians may conclude that Canadians have good reason to thank our federal-provincial controversies of recent decades for giving us the Charter which helps us respond to larger concerns than were on the minds of the participants. They will doubtless also conclude that the Charter is not enough, and that it is not an unalloyed good. Only political children, however, could have thought otherwise.

CHAPTER THREE

The Charter and the Constitution Act, 1982

The meaning of major constitutional change, such as the Constitution Act of 1982, is determined not exclusively by its contents but also by the interaction of the latter with a complex intellectual and political process that involves many actors and that goes on for decades. Such a change, it must also be remembered, is a supplement to an ongoing constitutional order with its own intellectual histories and embedded practices. To some extent, therefore, the new addition must be thought of as a graft that may not take, especially if it departs considerably from long-established constitutional assumptions.

In practical terms, the most important roles in determining the operational meaning of the new constitutional arrangements are played by the politicians and bureaucrats who work the recently modified system. Thus the meaning of the 1982 amending formula has acquired a specificity from its Meech Lake employment that was not immediately apparent. It is now clear, for example, that Part v, sections 38–49, Procedure for Amending Constitution of Canada, requiring authorizing resolutions by the legislatures of the agreeing governments, is not a mere formality but, in certain circumstances, may be a formidable hurdle.

Judges, of course, in interpreting the constitution establish precedents applicable to particular clauses and also develop more general philosophies to guide and constrain them in their task of judging. By simple observation of judicial behaviour, we now know that the Charter will not be a relative dead-letter, as was the 1960 Bill of Rights, but will be taken seriously by a Supreme Court cognizant that post-Charter Canada was intended to be recognizably different from pre-Charter Canada.

The intellectual and practical work of judges, politicians, and bureaucrats in influencing constitutional futures is supplemented by the ongoing intellectual and scholarly commentary of what may be called the interpretive community. This interdisciplinary community, with the legal professoriate playing a lead role, complemented by an emerging group of journalistic commentators, helps to shape the understandings that influence those with more direct responsibilities as well as the less involved mass citizenry which has little time for constitutional niceties.

The task of interpreting major constitutional changes, such as that of 1982, is never ended. Similar debates about the original Confederation agreement of the 1860s have livened the pages of many a scholarly journal and the speech of many a politician in the last century, and they continue to thrive. We endlessly debate such questions because they are the medium through which we redefine our past, present, and future as a people.

This chapter, therefore, is one more contribution to the collective self-examination of the most important constitutional change since Confederation, a non-incremental change driven by the desire to produce a new constitutional foundation for Canada.

As a package, the Constitution Act of 1982 brought about patriation of the Canadian constitution, contained a comprehensive set of amending formulae that freed Canadians from the humiliating requirement of requesting Westminster to pass legislation bringing about major constitutional change, included a Charter of Rights and Freedoms that repudiated the historic principle of parliamentary supremacy on which Canada had been founded, recognized and affirmed aboriginal and treaty rights, committed the governments and legislative bodies of Canada to the principle of equalization and the reduction of regional disparities, and extended provincial jurisdiction with respect to "Non-Renewable Natural Resources, Forestry Resources and Electrical Energy." Finally, in section 52(1), the Constitution Act contained a supremacy clause: "The Constitution of Canada is the supreme law of Canada, and any law that is inconsistent with the provisions of the Constitution is, to the extent of the inconsistency, of no force or effect."

With such a large and ambitious package, I have no alternative but to concentrate on the fundamentals – the severing of ties with the United Kingdom, the way in which the Charter redefines us as a people, and how it fits into an order hitherto primarily defined by parliamentary government and federalism. Beyond underlining the general magnitude of the change occasioned by the Charter, I hope to convince the reader that the 1982 compromise between, to simplify, the federally sponsored Charter and an amending formula fashioned by and sympathetic to provincial governments is not stable. If

Lord Durham were to revisit Canada now, he might report the existence of two competing visions warring in the bosom of the constitution.

The following chapter, on Meech Lake, will be devoted to the tension between these competing visions, a citizen-regarding Charter
and a government-regarding amending formula, that the Constitution Act of 1982 left to future generations to reconcile. Admittedly,
some degree of internal tension and discordant visions in a constitution may well be functional, in that subsequent generations will not
experience such a constitution as yesterday's limiting strait-jacket.
However, when the competing visions impair the effective working
of the constitution, their clashing coexistence is not a cause for con-
gratulation. This, I believe, is the case of the Constitution Act, 1982.

THE CONTEXT OF
INTERPRETATION

As the creation of the Constitution Act of 1982 recedes into history,
as we adapt to its consequences, and as the immediate passions that
attended its difficult birth subside, the controversies that preceded
its enactment give way to new ones about the meaning and evaluation
of what was achieved.

A dispassionate, clinical analysis of the virtues and shortfalls of
1982 is not to be expected, for competing evaluations of the Constitution Act became weapons in the subsequent constitutional debate
over the Meech Lake round. Indeed, the mere existence of Meech
Lake, both as substance and as process, provides an indelible contrast
with the Constitution Act that cannot be expunged from our memories as we try and discern the latter's meaning and significance in
our constitutional history. For Quebec's government and its supporters, for example, as for the Mulroney government that managed the
Meech Lake process, Meech Lake was a welcoming response to Quebec that contrasts with the latter's betrayal in 1982. For the élites of
various citizens' groups who acquired a taste for constitutional participation in the 1980–81 process, Meech Lake was castigated as an
unacceptable return to the dark ages when constitutional change was
an affair of governments alone. From a provincial perspective, Meech
Lake was applauded as a salutary provincialist counterattack to a
claimed centralist bias of the 1982 act. Conversely, for those who view
the 1982 outcome as itself a reasonable balancing of the conflicting
centralist and provincialist pressures inherent in federalism, Meech
Lake appeared as a damaging one-sided concession to a rampant
provincialism not confined to Quebec.

We cannot escape from these constitutional cross-currents. To accept their coexistence as central components of our constitutional fabric is the beginning of wisdom. In fact, the constitution should be viewed not as having an existence independent of such controversies – as an entity around which disagreement swirls – but rather as an evolving blend of support for and criticism of its different parts. In the last analysis, the constitution is thought and judgment.

At the time of its successful negotiation and subsequent proclamation, the Constitution Act received little fanfare – *And No One Cheered*,[1] as the title of a well-known volume stated. Some critics, noting the opposing assumptions behind the amending formula and the Charter, criticized an act that contained both as suffering from Jekyll and Hyde contradictions. Others contrasted its contents with the innumerable more ambitious might-have-beens that had fallen by the wayside. Critics who had been caught up in the excitement of the process and who had been led to believe that a more comprehensive package of change was possible viewed the limited 1982 achievement by the political agents of our reconfederation as a meagre outcome for so much effort. The limited change achieved fully satisfied none of the agreeing governments, was angrily rejected by the government of Quebec, received only tepid praise from the scholarly community of English Canada, and elicited bitterness, incredulity, and spiritual exhaustion from the nationalist Québécois intelligentsia. Even for many of the citizens' groups – the civil rights constituency, women, aboriginals, and "multiculturals" – the constitutional recognitions they had won shed little positive aura at the time over the total package of the Constitution Act. Their victories appeared more as grudging concessions extracted from flinty-eyed opponents than as rights and recognitions graciously granted because of their indisputable justice.

For some observers, the manner of the Constitution Act's arrival clouded its legitimacy – the infighting was too vicious and too public. The federal government's threat of unilateralism had not sat well with a population unused to Gaullist measures. The equivocal verdict of the Supreme Court on the unilateralist strategy seemed to imply a federal government prepared to employ constitutional immoralities not justified by raison d'état. Coupled with the reminder that the earlier proposals in Bill c-60 had also been struck down by the Supreme Court, it appeared to suggest a cavalier attitude to the old constitution, that might ill serve the prospects of its modified successor. Further, in the final days of frantic bargaining it was either deeply offensive or bitterly amusing to observe that the rights to be entrenched as a protection against the considered judgment of future legislatures could be altered by exhausted first ministers between breakfast and lunch. While public input into the hearings of the Special Joint Committee was, for many, a positive feature, it too was sullied by recognition that the extensive role accorded to the public was in considerable part a by-product of Ottawa's need for allies against the governments of the Gang of Eight dissenting provinces. At the time, the public role was often cynically described as a manipulated populism.

And of course, most crucial, there was the absence of the Quebec government from among the signing participants. The two decades of profound constitutional introspection that had been undertaken primarily in response to Québécois nationalism had concluded with the people of that province still deeply divided by the wrenching referendum experience and supporting a provincial government that claimed betrayal. From this perspective, the Constitution Act appeared both imperfect and incomplete, which suggested that, on some future, more auspicious occasion, an appropriate constitutional response to Quebec would have to be made.

These initial negative reactions seemed exaggerated in later years, at least up until Meech Lake. The gloomy predictions that Quebec's isolation would engender a renewed and tougher nationalism hardened by betrayal were not borne out. Even so, to offer, nearly a decade later, even qualified support for the 1982 outcome and the process from which it emerged may elicit the accusation levelled against some historians: that they always sided with the winners and employed a conceptual framework best described as Panglossian. However, the criteria from which our judgments emerge are not static. The initial negative assessments of those who did not cheer in and around 1982 were not informed by knowledge of later events: the resounding failure of a round of subsequent constitutional conferences to get agreement on aboriginal rights and the fact that Meech Lake, from its debut to its final act, never elicited more than a restrained half cheer, even from its supporters.

In retrospect, as the hostile reaction of many citizens' groups to Meech Lake makes clear, there is a striking degree of support for the Charter, as the major component of the Constitution Act of 1982, and of the relatively open process that produced it. In the light of Meech Lake, yesterday's criticisms of the relative lack of public input in the making of 1982 act have been silenced, to be replaced by appreciation of the degree of public involvement that did take place. In fact, the overall process leading up to the Constitution Act had much to recommend it. We can note at least four impressive factors.

1 - The Quebec government held a fair referendum, in 1980, on the future constitutional status of its people. Nearly all indications are that should Quebec have decided to become independent, on the basis of a second referendum following failure to negotiate sovereignty-association, the rest of Canada would have acquiesced. From the time the Parti québécois took office in 1976 until its defeat in 1985, there was negligible discussion of the use of force to keep a reluctant Quebec in a Confederation its people might wish to leave. Further, the PQ accepted with good grace the decisive results of a referendum that shattered the hopes of party members. In sum, Canadians within and outside Quebec debated peacefully the breakup of the country and appeared willing to live with whatever outcome emerged. This was a remarkable tribute by Canada's governments and peoples to the virtues of open discussions and democratic processes.

2 - On two significant issues, when the constitutional propriety of proposed federal actions was questionable, the courts were called on for judgment. In both cases – dealing with the proposal Senate reforms of Bill C-60 and the later patriation resolution – the Supreme Court's decisions were accepted by the politicians. In the latter case, the complicated decision induced the battling contestants to return to the bargaining table from which emerged the compromise embodied in the Constitution Act.

3 - Partly because it served the strategic interests of the federal government, the Special Joint Committee of 1980–1 that examined the federal government's proposed unilateralist package became a vehicle for extensive public input that significantly changed the Charter. Further, aboriginals and the women's movement reinstated, by mobilization, protections that had been removed in the final stages of bargaining.

4 - The Constitution Act had the support of ten of eleven governments and, because of the Charter, of the élites of most groups that had participated in the process. Although the act fell far short of responding to all the major demands that had been on the table, it was the most extensive change to our constitutional arrangements since Confederation. Further, it had the broadest base of popular support for any package of constitutional change in Canadian history, not excluding Confederation itself. It responded to provincial demands with the amending formula and the resources amendment and to Ottawa's preferences with an entrenched Charter, which also attracted extensive public support in English Canada.

THE RESULTING ACT has transformed Canada's constitutional culture much more profoundly than was anticipated. Public involvement in its making, the mini-histories that have grown up around the successful participation role of particular groups, and the constitutional identities that the Charter granted to women and others changed the relation of the written constitution to Canadian society. As I have argued elsewhere, "while federalism may still be largely about governments, federalism itself has lost relative status in the Constitution as an organizing principle. The Constitution is now also about women, aboriginals, multicultural groups, equality, affirmative action, the disabled, a variety of rights, and so on."[2] As a result, the traditional view of governments – that the constitution is primarily an instrument to regulate their affairs and that the management of formal constitutional change can therefore safely and properly be left to them – is anachronistic. It is challenged by a counterview that the constitution is also, via the Charter, a possession of the citizenry who accordingly should be participants in constitution-making.

This shift in the sources of constitutional legitimacy has redefined who are appropriate participants in formal changes to the constitution. This shift, inchoate and still of an indeterminate extent, clouds evaluations of the Constitution Act. In terms of traditional assumptions about legitimacy – namely, the quite proper dominance of governments in constitutional change – more than a taint of illegitimacy attends the 1982 outcome because of the Quebec government's negative response. However, in terms of newer notions of legitimacy, derived in large part from the 1982 act, extensive support for the Charter by rights-bearing citizens gives the Act a strong endorsement.

To assess the Constitution Act in terms of the federalism dynamic that put it on the agenda biases evaluation toward the negative, because of Quebec's exclusion. Further, our judgment is almost certainly biased by the fact that governments retain formal control of the amending formula. They define the problems that amendments are designed to resolve and by so doing pass judgment on the constitutional inheritance they are seeking to modify. It was almost inevitable, therefore, that the Meech Lake attempt to rectify what Quebec's government portrayed as the betrayal of the Québécois by the Constitution Act would not describe the latter positively. In general, within the operating units of government most directly involved, including the offices of premiers and Prime ministers and intergovernmental affairs units, the newer concerns of what might be called the Charter constituency appear to have limited salience compared to the more traditional interests of governments.

This bias within and among governments, however, may now be counterproductive, for it offends the women, the disabled, multicultural Canadians, and so on who see positive features in the 1982 outcome that they wish to protect and build on. Hence, as discussed below, the Meech Lake attempt to bring (the government of) Quebec back into the constitutional family through the use of executive federalism assumed what was no longer true: an unchallenged government monopoly of constitutional change subject only to the presumably ineffectual check of legislative approval. A purely intergovernmental response to Quebec that would have been consonant with constitutional norms in 1980–2 had become discordant with the emerging norms that sprang directly from the 1982 act. One's evaluation of the latter, therefore, inescapably colours appraisal of Meech Lake. Conversely, one's position on the latter logically implies a judgment on the Constitution Act, 1982. The Meech Lake controversy may thus be viewed as the scene of a conflict between still potent, but weakening traditional norms that make governments the agents of constitutional change and emergent norms, as yet uncrystallized, that suggest a vital public role. How a reconciliation will be worked out, and employing what arrangements, is among the most fundamental constitutional questions confronting Canadians.

CUTTING TIES WITH THE UNITED KINGDOM

Patriation of the BNA Act was the culmination of a long history of Canadian advances to ever-greater autonomy. The act of patriation made the constitution truly Canadian, alterable by Canadians employing known rules devised by Canadians.

From one perspective, this was a limited achievement: the continuing British role had been assumed only reluctantly by the United Kingdom's government for half a century. It was a vestigial survivor of a former colonial status that had lingered because of Canadians' inability to agree on an amending formula that they could operate themselves. Further, from the Canada–United Kingdom perspective, the tie-cutting was not a revolutionary repudiation of our past or of the former mother country. The constitutional monarchy remains at both federal and provincial levels, and much of our parliamentary practice continues to draw inspiration from Westminster. In addition, for many Canadians of British background, the United Kingdom continues to be "not a country like the others." Nevertheless, as our population becomes less British by origin, and our constitution less British by inspiration, patriation can be seen as a decisive, long-delayed symbolic step that will accelerate the adaptation of Canadians to their North American location and their increasingly multicultural, multiracial population. Patriation reflects and contributes to the relative decline in the domestic status of Canadians of British background. They no longer enjoy privileged status as connecting links to an imperial tradition. They are no longer Britons overseas, no longer members of Greater Britain, for whom it was plausible to assume the identity of British Canadians, with psyches split by a duality of allegiance to and identification with Great Britain and Canada simultaneously.

In this larger sense, it is easier to underestimate than to overestimate the constitutional importance of patriation. Patriation means that Canadians are now definitively on their own in North America and in the world. Symptomatic of the diminishing constitutional hold of our British past is the fact that the Charter that accompanied patriation gave Canadians a constitution "dissimilar in principle to that of the United Kingdom." Equally symptomatic has been the increasing constitutional and policy recognition accorded to Canada's non-British population. From the 1960s onward, dualism has always meant reducing anglophone dominance of public life, of the constitution, and of the national identity in order to enhance the recognition of francophones. This tendency was furthered by the Constitution Act, 1982, with its references to aboriginals, to "the multicultural heritage of Canadians," and to "race, national or ethnic origin [and] colour" in section 15 of the Charter. This constitutional underlining of Canadian ethnic heterogeneity was part of a diffuse decline in the Britishness of the constitution.

The declining significance of our British constitutional origins involved in patriation generates a need for indigenous constitutional theorizing and removes a barrier to its emergence. By leaving the power to amend the constitution in British hands in 1867, the Fathers of Confederation provided only an interim answer to the basic question a self-governing people must ultimately address: where sovereignty should reside. Our delay in answering that question not only testified to our political immaturity but also damaged the quality of our constitutional thought. Thus, disputes over Westminster's role, including the controversies over whether a residual trustee role gave the British government any discretion in responding to a Canadian request for an amendment, sometimes distracted Canadians from the substance of proposed changes. For example, debate over the substance of what became the Constitution Act of 1982 was partly sidetracked by a procedural debate over the constitutional propriety of the federal government's proposed request to Westminster and over the extent, if any, of surviving discretion in the British response.

Provincial governments opposed to the Charter were largely able to avoid discussing its alleged deficiencies by challenging in the courts and in the United Kingdom the unilateral procedure that Ottawa threatened to employ.

More serious, the kind of constitutional people we should become was a fundamental question we delayed in answering because a British role lingered for too long. For example, up to 1982, Canadian theorizing on a purely domestic amending procedure was conducted almost exclusively in terms of federalism and its governments. The need "to traipse over" to the United Kingdom was offensive to "a growing sense of Canadian nationalism," as Russell notes, and "meant that Canadians had not arrived at a consensus on where constitutional sovereignty should reside in their autonomous community."[3] Unfortunately, the context in which the sovereignty question was framed tended to structure the answers it elicited. Since the major controversial issue was the relative roles of Ottawa and the provinces in formulating and supporting an amendment request to Westminster, it was perhaps natural to think of amending procedures primarily in terms of relations among, and relative powers of, governments. Thus, the long history of Canadian efforts to eliminate the United Kingdom's role was dominated by the issue of the relative roles of the two orders of government in the purely domestic arrangements that would replace it. This context may help explain the failure of Pierre Trudeau's referendum proposals to "take."

In the same way as the pre-1949 role of the Judicial Committee inhibited development of indigenous jurisprudence – by deflecting attention to the national/imperial question of the role of British judges in Canadian constitutional evolution – the British role in constitutional amendment deflected attention from the essential domestic question of the location of sovereignty within Canada. When the debate was raised, concerns of federalism dominated, because a discourse of intergovernmental competition blanketed the Canadian debate. It now appears, in the light of Meech Lake, that the answer provided by the rules for amendment in the Constitution Act is at best transitional. It reflects the imperial context out of which the rules emerged and the pre-Charter climate in which they were fashioned. However, now that the imperial context is history and the Charter has arrived, another round of the debate on where constituent power should reside within Canada is appropriate, and it has in fact tentatively begun. Canadians will not immediately or easily do justice to the significance of this debate, for we are ill-equipped by our history to grapple with its subtleties. It is, however, a debate that cannot be avoided.

REARRANGING THE PUZZLE

The Charter of Rights joins a historic constitutional system whose two previous pillars have been parliamentary government and federalism. A functional coexistence of these three fundamental organizing principles must be worked out in the context of the complete Canadian autonomy that flows from the Constitution Act, 1982. Although the Charter builds on the weak precedent of John Diefenbaker's Bill of Rights, it is much more than an incremental step in Canadian constitutional evolution. The existence of the override, or notwithstanding clause (section 33), which allows a government, federal or provincial, to exempt any of its legislation in whole or in part from Charter clauses dealing with fundamental freedoms, legal rights, and equality rights, only marginally diminishes the constitutional discontinuity precipitated by the Charter.

The "notwithstanding clause" obviously has a lesser constitutional potency than the Charter itself, only some of whose provisions can be by-passed for renewable five-year terms by the vehicle of section 33's escape clause. The Charter is routinely applied by courts, while the notwithstanding clause is an extraordinary measure requiring special justification for its use, and legislative action for its implementation, which may elicit extensive public criticism.

The Charter modifies the practice of parliamentary government by the constraints that it imposes on legislatures and executives whose behaviour is subjected to a regime of judicially enforced Charter rights. At the same time, it reins in the federal dimension by setting Canadian limits to the scope and nature of diversities that legislative and executive power in the provinces can foster.

The constitutional change precipitated by the Charter is not to be viewed as analogous to the discrete addition of a new element, like a new detached garage, that coexists alongside but is not organically linked to the living arrangements that preceded its arrival. Rather, the appropriate perspective is that of the anthropologist observing a tribe whose traditional arrangements governing the status, power, rights, and duties of the paramount chief, elders, witch doctors, and ordinary tribespeople are irrevocably transformed through introduction of a new moral and spiritual order by recently arrived Christian missionaries. In such a case, the institutions and office-holders of the old order are pulled in new directions, although conversion to the new is always partial and restrained by the inertial weight of tradition.

At the same time, the missionaries cannot be entirely indifferent to the tribal ethos into which they have brought their message. Both consciously and unconsciously they will refine their message in order to reduce unnecessary dissonance with the recipient society. Within the tribe, response to the new message will vary. If the witch doctors cannot be co-opted, they will almost certainly be opposed and will fight rearguard battles appealing to the sacred origins of what is under attack. The responses of the great chief and of the elders may vary depending on how the new message affects power relations among them. The former, whose agreement was a prerequisite to the willing reception of the missionaries in the first place, may redefine himself as a modernizing chief and thus reduce the attention he pays to the elders and the ancient tribal wisdom they command. The ordinary tribespeople may be especially responsive to the universalism and egalitarianism of the new message that might, if properly exploited, elevate their status by undermining traditional hierarchical inequalities based on immemorial custom.

What analogous reshuffling of status, power, institutional interdependencies, basic values, and citizen and élite identities might strike an anthropologist who turns to a Canada adapting to the Charter for somewhat novel subject matter?

The Enhanced Status of the Constitution

The Constitution Act of 1982 elevates the status of the constitution itself in several distinct ways. Technically, a new status is symbolized by section 52(1), which declares the constitution to be "the supreme law of Canada, and any law that is inconsistent with the provisions of the Constitution is, to the extent of the inconsistency, of no force or effect." Psychologically, given the diminished positive symbolism attached to the British connection in the late twentieth century, patriation extricated the constitution from the derivative, colonial aura that had clung to the BNA acts, the basic components of the written constitution. Further, the Charter gave the written constitution, now domiciled in Canada, a public presence that the BNA Act had always lacked. It linked Canadians directly to the constitution by the vehicle of rights. In particular, it gave constitutional niches or identities to women, aboriginal Canadians, official-language minorities, visible minorities and third-force Canadians, and all those singled out for special mention in the equality rights clauses of sections 15(1) and (2).

The élites of these various groups quickly developed a certain proprietary attitude to the instrument that raised their status, and thus indirectly to the constitution of which it was a part. They were thus induced to think of themselves as having a constitutional presence and therefore of being legitimate constitutional actors. Precisely what these developments might mean in the future was unclear in 1982, beyond the new truism that the constitution, via the Charter, is a much more visibly comprehensive instrument than formerly, that it now reaches overtly, deeply, and selectively into Canadian society, and that, accordingly, its enhanced symbolism is integrally linked to a constitutional readjustment of the relative status of governments and citizens, to the advantage of the latter.

The Transformation of Constitutional Discourse

As numerous authors have observed, the Charter generates a dialogue on citizen-state relations that is an alternative to the federal-provincial discourse that emerges in an almost Pavlovian fashion from the élites of the federal system who govern Canadians. Considerable time will be required before the varied expressions of this new dialogue become clear. Its basic focus will be on rights and freedoms, with consequently higher visibility for citizen-state relations, now and hereafter subject to never-ending, high-profile public dialogue. A legal discourse will culminate in ex cathedra judicial decisions that will authoritatively declare the actual meaning of "the supreme law of Canada" for the case at hand. It is strikingly evident, however, that a rights discourse has escaped the confines of the legal process and is insinuating itself into everyday political activity. Most important, for our analysis, a rights orientation strengthens expectations among opinion leaders of the varied Charter clientele groups that their voices should be heard on matters that directly affect their interests. For constitutional issues, the Charter will probably weaken deference to governing élites and enhance self-confidence among those who carry Charter identities as possessors of rights.

Constitutional discourse triggered by the Charter, however, will not be restricted to rights narrowly defined. An ethnic discourse has developed that debates the relative status to be accorded to the two "founding" British and French peoples and the later arrivals who have made Canadians a multicultural and multiracial people.[4] A different, though related, and very complex discourse seeks to determine the appropriate relationship of the Indian, Inuit, and Métis peoples – now constitutionally defined as the "aboriginal peoples of Canada" – to the larger community and to governments. Aboriginal constitutional discourse explores the extent to which and the manner in which aboriginal peoples should possess rights and duties of citizenship unique to themselves. Yet another discourse given sustenance by the Charter, especially its guaranteeing of the Charter's "rights and freedoms ... equally to male and female persons" in section 28, focuses on the appropriate constitutional consequences of male/female differences and on the constitution's potential to alleviate sex-based inequalities.

With the partial exception of the special aboriginal discourse, these emergent thematic perspectives foster a national dialogue. They define Canadians by means of differences and socio-ethnic categories that transcend provincial boundaries. A decline in the relative incidence of provincial orientations in political, including constitutional, rhetoric is a necessary consequence.

The Enhanced Status of Citizenship

One of the most significant constitutional consequences of the Charter has attracted little attention – its enhancement of the institution of citizenship. There are at least three reasons for this inadequate attention.

First, citizenship has always been a thin concept in Canadian constitutional and political analysis. Our founding as a distinct people in 1867 was an élite phenomenon that did nothing to stress the future role of citizens in the country about to be born. For decades after Confederation, many Canadians of British origin continued to think of themselves as having a dual civic identity and loyalty – to Canada and to the mother country and the empire it governed. The process of acquiring Canadian citizenship, given the absence of a Canadian creed at least prior to the Charter, was never endowed with the "rite of passage" significance available to prospective Americans in analogous circumstances. Thus, the explicit language of citizenship was not prominent in the creation of the Charter and was not easily available for making sense of this new instrument.

Second, the language of the Charter only sporadically engages the concept of citizenship. Its rights and freedoms are not restricted to citizens only but, depending on the right or freedom in question, are guaranteed to "Everyone," "Any person," "Anyone," "Every individual," and "Any member of the public," as well as to "Every Citizen," and "Citizens of Canada." The fact that the Charter's benefits are not confined to citizens, with its corollary that much of the Charter does not appear to elevate citizens above non-citizens, leads easily to the conclusion that the citizenship consequences of the Charter are negligible. This, however, is to restrict inappropriately the significance of citizenship to the distinctions it creates among the general public of citizens and non-citizens alike. What does the Charter do to and for the status of citizens vis-à-vis governments? What does the Charter do to and for the role of citizenship as such in the constitutional order? The answers are not given by the reading of constitutional texts, although the rights and freedoms available to "Everyone," and so on, are by definition available to citizens and thus enrich the possession of rights that citizens enjoy.

Third, the impact of the Charter on conceptions of citizenship is indirect. The Charter's rights and freedoms are ubiquitous reminders that the base of the constitutional order is composed not of subjects but of rights-bearing citizens on whose behalf the business of government is undertaken. The changes in constitutional culture to which this leads, Robert Vipond astutely argues, bring to the surface hitherto dormant questions as to the locus of sovereignty in Canada.[5] The answer given by the 1982 amending formula – that sovereignty resides in governments which are given exclusive charge of amending the constitution, subject to legislative ratification – is not easily accommodated to a Charter-influenced constitutional culture. The Charter denies ownership of the constitution to governments and, by reminding the citizenry that it possesses rights as a protection against governments in ordinary times, inevitably suggests an equivalent need for protection against governments seeking formal changes to the constitution. Although American experience suggests that a Bill of Rights and an amending process based on initiation by Congress and approval by state legislatures can long cohabit the same system, recent Canadian experience has suggested a tension within a constitution that both protects Canadians against governments by means of a Charter and, as in Meech Lake, informs governments that they can amend the constitution, including the Charter, with as little public input as they can get away with. This difference between the two countries may reflect the facts that both the Charter and the amending formula are constitutional newcomers which Canadians are still learning to work, that the Charter was not welcomed by most provincial governments, and that projects of further constitutional reform have had a very high profile since the 1982 act.

The Charter and Federalism

The Charter constrains the parliamentary supremacy of both orders of government, although both federal and provincial governments have access to section 33's notwithstanding clause, which allows legislation to stand that would otherwise be in conflict with a provision in section 2 or sections 7 to 15 of the Charter. However, the Charter's impartiality does not extend to its relative impact on the central and provincial governments. For the latter, every time the Charter nullifies a provincial executive or legislative action, it limits provincial variations in policy and administrative behaviour by invoking Canadian values. In a competition between a Charter-sustained Canadian value and a provincial value, the latter will lose. By contrast, Charter nullification of a federal executive or legislative act is an affirmation of Canadian values and thus strengthens a discourse that defines Canadians in other than provincial terms, an outcome that cannot be entirely displeasing to Ottawa.

This asymmetrical relation of the Charter to Canadian federalism explains several historical developments: Ottawa's advocacy since the late 1950s of an entrenched Charter binding on both orders of government; the provinces' support for parliamentary supremacy in the last quarter-century, for no Charter or a weak Charter, and for a capacious "reasonable limits" clause, which would, in effect, weaken the Charter's protection of rights (and was, in response to public pressure, resisted by Ottawa);[6] the role of the notwithstanding clause as a concession to placate dissenting provinces opposed to the Charter; post-1982 use of the notwithstanding clause solely by provincial governments; and recent heavy pressure for the clause's elimination from the national parties in the federal parliament. Such a pattern is not accidental. It derives from the Charter's interaction with a federal system whose two orders of governments accord different weights to territorially based particularisms and country-wide uniformity of treatment.

Courts and Legislatures

Some scholars resist the argument that the Charter sets courts and legislatures against each other. Much of the alleged conflict, they suggest, vanishes when it is recognized that most Charter cases involve the conduct of public officials, typically the police – a consideration that greatly weakens the democratic critique of judicial review. In a more complex thesis, W.R. Lederman argues that the activities of courts and legislatures are not competitive, but complementary, in the sense that both are obligated to respect the Charter.[7] Samuel LaSelva makes a similar point: if legislators were indifferent to constitutionality and were influenced only by "utilitarian and majoritarian considerations, while only judges based their decisions upon the constitution, then our constitutional polity would come to an end."[8]

These arguments are both significant and correct. It is a necessary assumption of constitutional government that governments are law-abiding, not rogue elephants hostile by nature to any limitations on their conduct. The limited judicial scrutiny that courts can apply to legislation and to executive behaviour suggests that constitutional norms would not survive if adherence to them by legislatures and executives were based entirely on fear of judicial detection of their violation.

However, the internal constraints on the use of the notwithstanding clause suggested by LaSelva, or the complementarity between courts and legislatures referred to by Lederman, both necessarily refer to the behaviour of governing élites after the Charter was implemented. The complementarity, especially from Lederman's perspective, describes the terms of coexistence or co-operation worked out between courts and legislatures after the Charter has redefined the boundaries of permissible action by the latter.

In fact, of course, the argument that courts and legislatures, as well as cabinet ministers, senior administrators, and traffic cops, have all internalized the norms of the Charter is powerful testimony to its ability to change both beliefs and behaviour.[9] Sterling Lyon and other defenders of parliamentary supremacy clearly saw that introduction of a Charter was a major departure from the historic British tradition self-consciously continued at Confederation. The philosophies of entrenched rights and of parliamentary supremacy derive from divergent political traditions. A regime historically founded on the latter is profoundly transformed by introduction of a Charter, the central institutional expression of the former.

The special responsibility of courts in this new regime is to flesh out the constitutional norms that will be voluntarily adhered to by those who are subject to the Charter's requirements, clearly including legislatures and executives. The judicial role is perhaps best thought of not as policing boundaries to prevent infractions but as falling somewhere between teaching and preaching in order to mould the future behaviour of those with whom they share the task of fulfilling the Charter's mandate.

The Enhanced Status of the Supreme Court

The higher status of the constitution necessarily adds to the responsibilities of the body that undertakes its final interpretation. The traditional institution that gains most in status, visibility, and influence as a result of the Charter, therefore, is the judiciary – most notably, the Supreme Court, with its de facto and symbolic leadership role. To its role as umpire between provinces and Ottawa is added its even more visible obligation of arbitrating relations between citizens and the state. Traditional concerns about its composition, the appointment process, and the jurisprudence that should govern its decisions all appear in a new guise. It is no longer adequate to address these issues almost exclusively from the vantage point of the division of powers, and therefore of federalism, and thus to ignore the impact of the Charter on them.[10] The new constitutional actors created by the Charter also care about all the factors that enter into judicial decisions. Thus proposals for Supreme Court reform that are restricted to pre-Charter concerns defined primarily by federalism are likely to fall short of or overlook new agendas for reform raised by the Charter.

The generally increased importance in Canadian life of the constitution – and hence of the judiciary – gives more influence within governments to departments of justice and attorney-generals' ministries. Their internal advice-giving roles expand, concurrent with their growing external responsibility for defending their governments in courtrooms. The overall result is to add to the already substantial influence of lawyers in public life.

THE CHARTER TAKES ROOT

It is not easy to predict the long-run impact of the Charter of Rights on Canada's national and provincial communities. The Charter applies to a people, shaped by more than a century of life together, who have learned to work the institutions of parliamentary government and federalism. It will, along with other factors, modify the civic identities of Canadians, but its full impact will not be apparent for several decades, although a remarkable adoption of a rights language is already apparent.[11]

In marked contrast to the limited vision of the 1960 Bill of Rights, the Charter is a generous, eclectic document. It brings together and consolidates the outcomes of many of the previous quarter-century's struggles for rights, status, and recognition.[12] While the Charter has "elevated the status of the Canadian *people* vis-à-vis our governments,"[13] its description of that people is far from simple. To some extent, it is a Janus-faced document, presenting both liberal individualism and a constitutionalization of the linguistic, ethnic, racial, cultural, and sex identities of Canadians. The former approach is found in the more traditional fundamental freedoms, democratic rights, and legal rights. The latter is expressed in the Charter's singling out of official language minorities (section 23), Canadians' multicultural heritage (section 27), sex (section 28), and aboriginals (section 25 – as well as section 35 of the Constitution Act). Nine abstract groupings in the equality provisions of section 15 of the Charter, ranging from race to physical disability, supplement these categorizations.

These coexisting thematic thrusts provide the basis for competing attributions of where the Charter's essence lies. To John Whyte, who identifies Trudeau's goal as a "modern liberal nation marked by a single fundamental relationship between the polity and individual citizens," the Charter will make the citizen-state relationship "systematized, centralized, uniform, constant, unilateral and direct," in marked contrast to that relation in federalism – "diverse, filtered, diluted, subject to mediation, and complicated."[14] Scholars who write from the perspectives of critical legal studies, Marxism, or a generally social-democratic tendency agree that the Charter is a liberal individualist document, but they see its arming of "individuals with a negative set of formal rights to repel attempts at government interference"[15] as an unfortunate constraint on the state's capacity to alleviate injustices of the market-place. The Charter's private rights produce public wrongs.[16] The most important thing about the Charter, according to Andrew Petter, "is that it is, at root, a 19th century document set loose on a 20th century welfare state."[17] To other critics of the Charter, such as Charles Taylor, the emphasis on individual rights not only atomizes society but, with its nationalizing, levelling propensities, is destructive of the smaller communities on which Canada is allegedly based and therefore hostile to the goal of a participatory democratic culture which cannot flourish in a continental community of rights-bearers.[18]

Others deny the Charter's exclusive liberal individualism, by stressing its "ideological heterodoxy"[19] or by noting that its liberal individualist rhetoric coexists with an emphasis on communitarian values.[20] David Elkins, in his recent presidential address to the Canadian Political Science Association, differentiates the Canadian Charter and the US Bill of Rights by stressing the former's collective or group rights which are conspicuously absent from the latter.[21] Those who write in this vein point to minority-language education rights, aboriginal rights, multiculturalism, and denominational school rights as indicators of a group, collective, or communitarian orientation in the Charter. To Thomas Berger, an eloquent exponent of this view, the Charter is a response to the historic French-English duality of Canada, to the aboriginal peoples, and to our multiethnicity. He sees the essence of the Charter in its recognition, affirmation, and protection of diversity.[22]

The Charter's inclusion of the categories cited by Berger unquestionably testifies to the distance that Canadians have travelled since the not-too-distant time when Indians did not have the vote, the francophone side of duality was only weakly expressed in national affairs and institutions, non-founding peoples had a low profile, and multiracial considerations were for other nations, not Canadians. From this perspective, the Charter appears as almost a compendium of the group basis of our existence. Its social vision is incorporative and pluralistic rather than levelling. And while the Charter's individual rights may be its dominant theme, that theme is attenuated by a miscellany of group recognitions and entitlements that are immensely varied, ranging from positive entitlements to the receipt of particular services (section 23, minority-language educational rights) to a requirement that the Charter's interpretation is to be consistent with "the multicultural heritage of Canadians" (section 27).

The burgeoning literature that fleshes out these competing assessments may be taken as testimony to the Charter's eclecticism – or to its damaging ambiguities. Politically, however, the literature of controversy confirms that the Charter is taking root. In a few years, it has acquired an infrastructure of scholarship that makes it almost impossible to visualize the document in the more pristine state when it first became part of the constitution in 1982. A recent bibliography of Charter publications up to August 1988, seventy-eight pages in length, listed about 1,400 items.[23] The Charter has become an institution.

Ultimately, the evolution of the future blend of the individual and collective aspects of the Charter will be a product of law and politics, particularly given that Charter clauses relating to sex, language, ethnicity, and aboriginal status are able to generate organizations devoted to their protection or strengthening much more than are clauses relating to the more traditional individual rights, even with the impressive number of civil liberties organizations in Canada. In the same way as Quebec is not a province like the others, because it can mobilize a national sentiment behind its aspirations, some Charter clauses may also be unlike the others in their greater long-run political capacity to tap emotional reservoirs of support linked to the powerful stimuli of sex, language, and ethnicity.

IN RESPONDING TO THE CHARTER, our plural society has adapted across multiple fronts to the new constraints and opportunities that it offers. A flood of publications signifies the emergence of a scholarly infrastructure to support the bench in its awesome task. Law and political science, along with some other social sciences, are experiencing partial rapprochement and are sharing disciplinary skills to cope with the divergent but overlapping research concerns generated by the expanded role that the Charter gives to courts.

The Charter watch extends to the self-interested concern of Charter constituencies as to how courts' structure, personnel composition, and jurisprudence assist the groups' interests and perspectives. New litigation lobby groups, some with government funding, exploit the new opportunities to move policy in directions that the Charter creates. For example, a 1984 report for the Canadian Advisory Council on the Status of Women asserted that, with the Charter in place, "we find ourselves at the opportune moment to stress litigation as a vehicle for social change."[24]

Successive chief justices and other Supreme Court judges explore in public the implications of their new responsibilities and solicit the assistance of the academic community extending beyond the boundaries of law faculties.[25] The courts acknowledge that the Charter is not John Diefenbaker's Bill of Rights and should be treated differently.[26] Further, future judges raised in a Charter-influenced constitutional culture will, presumably, be less influenced by historic beliefs in parliamentary supremacy. In any event, that tradition has been weakened by a global and domestic rights consciousness and also by the diminished status of its originator, the United Kingdom. What Peter Russell calls the "*zeitgeist* of the legal community" takes the Charter seriously, an attitude reinforced by the widespread availability of legal aid.[27] Indeed, the legal community played a vanguard role in advocating the Charter and encouraging the Supreme Court to wield its new mandate vigorously.[28] A small cadre of journalists is emerging with a capacity to guide the lay person through the intricacies of Supreme Court decisions. Every few days the media report that some government or other is exploring the compatibility or conflict between some of its historic practices and Charter provisions.

In brief, there has been an impressive, multifaceted response to the requirements the Charter imposes on Canadians, much influenced by the conditioning of previous decades. The contribution of the United Nations to legitimating a rights-oriented discourse has already been noted. The Canadian Bill of Rights of 1960, despite its inadequacies, accustomed Canadians to living with such a code and thus minimized the discontinuity which the Charter would otherwise have brought. Also, Canadians live next door to a rights-oriented polity, and since the end of appeals to the Judicial Committee in 1949, the influence of the contrary British tradition on Canadian jurisprudence has diminished. Further, the Charter emerged out of a public process in which numerous civil liberties, ethnic, womens', and other groups lobbied vigorously for a strong document. The public was generally in favour, influenced partly by Ottawa's persuasive propaganda, which portrayed the Charter's opponents as self-interested and insensitive to rights.[29] The Charter was also the centrepiece of the federal response to a constitutional crisis that had racked the country for years, and hence a document to be taken seriously at the time and subsequently. The Charter already has a high public profile in a constitution hitherto characterized by very low visibility.

The Charter's framers clearly intended to limit the possibility that it would be trivialized by the courts or ignored by the public. Section 52 (1) states: "The Constitution of Canada is the supreme law of Canada, and any law that is inconsistent with the provisions of the Constitution is, to the extent of the inconsistency, of no force or effect." Section 24(1) explicitly gives enforcement power to the judiciary: "Anyone whose rights and freedoms, as guaranteed by this Charter, have been infringed or denied may apply to a court of competent jurisdiction to obtain such remedy as the court considers appropriate and just in the circumstances." The judiciary has clearly responded to this new mandate.

A few years ago, a leading scholar asserted that "Canadian judges have begun to carve out a bold new constitutional jurisprudence. Led by the Supreme Court, judges have stressed that the constitutional status of the Charter qualitatively distinguishes it from the statutory Bill of Rights of 1960" and that accordingly it should receive more generous interpretation.[30]

Thus, although the time span is too short for definitive judgments, the Charter appears to be taken seriously by relevant publics and by the courts. An analysis of the early Charter era, from 1982 through 1985, identified a "remarkably high degree of success" of approximately 31 per cent for Charter litigants.[31] As Peter Russell anticipated some time ago, the Charter has been employed much more vigorously by litigants to challenge public officials than to attack legislation.[32] Two out of three cases are what a recent study calls "conduct cases," about half of which involve police,[33] whose behaviour the courts may be keeping within the bounds set by their political superiors.

The impact of the Charter, however, cannot be determined by looking exclusively at the batting average of litigants in judicial proceedings. The Charter, after all, had political purposes as well: strengthening the national community, diminishing the salience of provincial cleavages, and supplementing the discourse focused on federalist definitions of issues with a counter-discourse relatively indifferent to territorialism and organized around rights. The hopes of Charter supporters are well summed up by Deborah Coyne, who credits it with "a subtle nationalizing effect as it gives expression to a national citizenship that is independent of territorial/regional location and that transcends regional identities [with] its appeal to our non-territorial identities – race, ethnicity, gender, age, and so forth."[34]

Sociologist Raymond Breton, reacting against an economism that defines the state's role primarily in terms of managing the economy, reminds Canadians of what Clifford Geertz more generally has argued – namely, the importance of the symbolic order to the collective life of a people.[35] The making of societies, Breton argues, is an unending task of constructing and revising the collective identities that get expressed in ideologies of peoplehood and in public symbols that strengthen identification with the political community. By these means, individuals find a correspondence between their private selves and official public representations of their community.[36]

In Canada, the Charter was intended to modify the symbolic order by linking individuals directly to the constitution by the vehicle of rights. The public judicial reiteration of the value of rights stimulates Canadians to view themselves as "rights-holders, thereby transforming the language of political discourse in Canada."[37] This rights discourse is not simply a detachable, instrumental language devoid of effects on those who employ it. On the contrary, it works on the mental maps we live by, by providing routes to destinations we formerly might not have thought of. As Marc Gold observes, one significant "conception of rhetoric [sees it] as the way in which we constitute ourselves as a community through language."[38]

In general, as Gibbins, Knopff, and Morton suggest, the pre-Charter Canadian constitution stimulated a jurisprudence that "mirrored and thus strengthened the dynamic of federal-provincial conflict as the organizing principle of the political process."[39] The Charter, however, allows individuals and groups that are indifferent to federalism to resist the latter's organizing imperative and to take issues directly to court, where the "crosscutting ideological formulation of such issues will be emphasized at the expense of any territorial dimension they may have."[40] Thus the Charter allows issues such as abortion, the death penalty, and numerous equality issues to be confronted as matters of constitutional principle in the judicial arena. In some areas, such as censorship and Sunday closing, the Supreme Court will be "establishing national standards applicable to all the provinces. Here we will see the centralizing tendency of the Charter at work. Historically with regard to both these matters, substantive decision-making was subject to a regime of provincial local option. Now the Supreme Court will serve as a national supervisor of legislative action with regard to these controversial subjects."[41] These divisive moral issues transcending federalism become Canadian issues and will be litigated as such. The debates they engender will constitute an ongoing lesson in Canadianism. The divisions they stimulate will be ideological and national, not regional. They will be debates culminating in the Canadian Supreme Court, about the meaning, boundaries, and protection of rights located in a Charter that applies to all Canadians.[42]

On the whole, the Charter portrays Canadians as a single national community with other than provincial distinctions. Admittedly, some sections of the Charter display provincial sensitivities. The override in section 33 and the mobility rights subsection, 6(4), allowing special programs for socially or economically disadvantaged individuals in a province with a rate of employment below the Canadian rate, are exceptions in deferring to provincialism, as also is section 59, which delays the coming into effect in Quebec of section 23(1)(a) until authorized by the legislative assembly or government of Quebec.[43]

These, however, are exceptions in a document that overwhelmingly defines the Canadian people in non-federal terms. The Charter's sections on minority-language educational rights obligate provincial governments to provide educational instruction in the minority official language. These sections sacrifice the rights of provincial majorities to determine language policy in educational settings in order to further a particular vision of the pan-Canadian community. The holders of such minority rights can judge the behaviour of provincial governments through the national lens provided by the Charter. This exemple, however, only illustrates the Charter's general tendency to take people psychologically out of their provincial communities. In that sense, at the level of the citizen, the Charter reduces the distinction between "section 91 Canada" and "section 92 Canada". Both orders of government now encounter rights-bearing Canadians – a modification more of the provincial political environment than of the federal.

Whether judicial application of the Charter will constrain provincial governments more than the federal is a different matter. However, recent empirical evidence covering all appeal court decisions from 1982 to 1988 suggests that the Charter not only is having a more pronounced effect on legislation than had been thought but also is restricting the autonomy of the provinces more than that of Parliament.[44] If this trend continues, suspicions about its anti-federal tendency will be further confirmed.

The judicial role in these decisions is clearly constitution-making. The vague generalities of the Charter have been likened to "limp balloons ... [and] ... the judges must decide how much air to blow into them, ... a constitution-making role" no less significant than the original creative role of the Charter's architects.[45] Over time, the cumulative decisions of courts jell into jurisprudential doctrine. Random behaviour is incompatible with the judicial office. The long-run tendency of decisions, accordingly, is to strive for philosophical coherence of the concepts under examination. When these concepts pertain to rights, and thus draw on a rich philosophical tradition, the goal is a comprehensive definition of a Canadian in terms of Charter rights.

The composite portrayal will always have imperfections, it will not stand still, and it will be contested. Nevertheless, future citizens will have a richer, more articulate, and more nuanced description available of what it is to be a Canadian. In other words, the Charter will not only judicialize our politics and politicize the judiciary as already argued,[46] but will also philosophize our collective identity. It will make Canadians a more theoretical people and will give judges much more say in the formation of their evolving collective self-definition. No doubt, the Canadian portrait as developed by the judiciary will be much more comprehensible to élites than to ordinary citizens, but that is simply a tautological reminder of what an élite is. (Note: This chapter was initially delivered as a lecture in early 1987. Chapter 4 presents a more recent assessment that profits from the Meech Lake experience and underlines the relative failure of the Charter to "take" among Quebec's francophone majority, especially its nationalist élites, as compared to English Canada.)

THE AMENDING FORMULA
AND THE CHARTER

From a historical perspective, the adoption of a domestic amending formula in the Constitution Act, 1982, agreed to by all governments but Quebec, was a major constitutional breakthrough. It put an end to a quest that had intermittently engaged Canadian governments since 1927. It eliminated a role for Westminster that had become as embarrassing to British as to Canadian politicians.

The 1982 amending formula is not simple; indeed, Peter Meekison speaks of amending formulae, for there are six different means to secure amendments, depending on the constitutional subject-matter and the governments involved.[47] With specified exceptions (section 41), the relevant provincial legislature can amend the constitution of a province (section 45); and, again with specified exceptions (sections 41 and 42), Parliament may amend the constitution of Canada with reference to the executive government of Canada or the Senate and House of Commons (section 44); an amendment that applies to one or more but not all provinces may be authorized by resolutions of Parliament and the legislative assemblies of the provinces to which it applies (section 43). For an amendment that requires provincial support, the approval of the House of Commons by resolution is sufficient, in the absence of Senate support, if the House adopts for the second time a resolution that it had already adopted more than 180 days previously (section 47).[48] An important list of subjects requires unanimous consent, including the various amending formulae themselves, (section 41).[49] And, most notably, the "general procedure" requires resolutions of both Houses of Parliament and "of the legislative assemblies of at least two-thirds of the provinces that have, in the aggregate, according to the then latest general census, at least fifty per cent of the population of all the provinces" (section 38). Further, a province may opt out of an amendment made under this section that "derogates from the legislative powers, the proprietary rights or any other rights or privileges of the legislature or government of a province" (section 38[2][3]). As Meekison states, "The principle of opting out is the cornerstone of the new amending formula."[50] Further, if a province opts out of an amendment transferring legislative jurisdiction from the provinces to the federal government, that province is entitled to "reasonable compensation" from Ottawa, if it is an amendment "relating to education or other cultural matters" (section 40).

For provincial governments, especially the seven remaining members of the Gang of Eight, following Quebec's unwillingness in November 1981 to accept the modifications insisted on by the federal government, the amending formula was a heady constitutional triumph. With some alterations,[51] it was the amending formula they had proposed in the package they released in April 1981 as their way out of the constitutional impasse. Appropriately, the sense of achievement was especially pronounced for the Lougheed government of Alberta, which had developed the formula.

The new formula, based on the "equality of the provinces," could be portrayed as an appropriate extension of the principles of federalism to a new arena. It could also be viewed as the political realists' acceptance of cabinet ascendancy or as simply recognizing the dominance of governments in executive federalism, where, presumably, future constitutional amendments would be thrashed out.

As Barry Strayer observed in a 1966 article, "the view which one takes of an amending procedure will largely depend on the concept he has of the nature and purpose of the constitution itself."[52] For provincial governments hostile to majoritarianism and to referendums, the formula reflected the historic assumption that the written constitution was mainly about federalism, an affair of governments; hence formal constitutional change should properly reside in the hands of governments. Thus the formula appeared to solidify government control of the amending formula and to have warded off the threatening prospect held out by Ottawa's proposals to give Canadian citizens, via referenda, a say in amending the constitution of their country.

There was one qualification to government (i.e. cabinet) dominance: the requirement of approving resolutions from the Senate, the House of Commons, and the legislative assemblies of provinces supporting the proposed amendment. While this was a modification of previous practice, in which executive approval sufficed, inexplicably there was no overt anticipation that this might be a serious hurdle rather than a ritual to be observed.

While the Gang of Eight's amending formula was in obvious conflict with the very different assumptions behind the federal government's preferred formula, it was, with a few modifications, grudgingly acceptable to Ottawa. It was a price that had to be paid to obtain sufficient provincial approval to go to Westminster with a package that included the Charter.

It is easy to get lost in or mesmerized by the details of current amending formulae and thus lose sight of the larger vision that lies behind them – and what that vision lacks. The amending formula derives from federalism to the exclusion of other concerns; the relevant actors in federalism for amending purposes are governments; the essential principle of federalism is the equality of the provinces; and the innovative principle of the formula is the opting-out provisions, which "guarantee to each and every province that constitutional amendments which derogate from their existing legislative powers, proprietary rights or other rights cannot be imposed upon them without their consent."[53]

The underlying philosophy is a product of the Gang of Eight, building on earlier proposals by Alberta, which fashioned the provincial Constitutional Accord that, slightly modified, became Part v of the Constitution Act, 1982. The accord was defensive, designed to protect provinces – which were equated with provincial governments – from nationalizing and centralizing pressures. It was based overwhelmingly on the interests of "provincial communities and provincial governments, with the latter endowed with indefeasible rights in perpetuity to the jurisdictional powers they possessed."[54] The document was unremittingly provincialist and precluded a national majority of governments or voters, no matter how large, from dictating amendments to a recalcitrant provincial government, except in matters pertaining to the House of Commons, the Senate, and the Supreme Court, the establishment of new provinces, and the extension of existing provinces into the territories. These matters, which did not affect provincial jurisdiction or proprietary or other rights, would be covered by the two-thirds and 50 per cent rule (i.e. Parliament plus legislatures of seven provinces representing at least half of Canada's population).

With these few exceptions, the accord gave individual governments the capacity to resist unwanted constitutional change without penalty. In explicitly repudiating any popular input by referenda, the accord was designed to protect the rights of each provincial government not only from other governments but also from its own people who, being Canadian citizens as well as provincial residents, might take a less provincialist view than their governments of future amendments they could be asked to approve. As Stephen Scott observed, and for the reasons just identified, even the Charter did not elicit "remotely as bitter a response from provincial authorities across the country as did the inclusion of the referendum process" in the federal proposals.[55] This provincial-government hostility was also stimulated by the form of the initial federal proposal, designed to serve Ottawa's interests, with minimum concession to subtlety. The provinces' government-centred view also accounts for the absence of reference to a Charter of Rights in the accord. A referendum procedure and a Charter would leave provincial governments vulnerable to Canadianizing tendencies among their own residents and to a philosophizing judiciary that might value the federal values of diversity less than protection of the Canadian rights contained in a Charter. The accord thus expressed a provincialist, governmentalist, protective philosophy. It sought to combine flexibility – with the two-thirds and 50 per cent rule as its basic formula – with iron-clad protection of provincial rights – opt-out plus compensation – at the cost of nation-wide uniform application of future amendments.[56]

The amending formula was refined in closed meetings of the eight governments least sympathetic to the Charter. The appropriateness of such an amending formula for a constitution that contained a potent Charter was not, therefore, a consideration for the sponsors.

The amending formula and its sponsors never directly confronted what might be called the Charter constituencies. The formula was not available for public scrutiny by the citizens' groups that sought to strengthen the Charter in the Special Joint Committee. The amending formula before that committee was the federal proposal, with its referendum component. By contrast, the Gang of Eight moved its formula through the formative stages protected from possible intrusions from an inquisitive and demanding citizenry. The latter thus would not recognize the "symbolic importance" of the amending formula or appreciate, as Charter supporters did a few years later, the clash between the premises that lay behind the Charter and those that were behind the provincialist, government-dominated amending formula that joined the Charter in the Constitution Act.[57]

When intergovernmental agreement on a slightly modified version of the provincialist amending formula was made public, it was part of a constitutional package that also contained encroachments on the rights that women and aboriginals thought they had already secured. As a result, in the few additional hectic weeks within which further change to the agreed package turned out to be possible, public attention and pressure were directed almost exclusively and successfully to reinstatement of what aboriginals and women had lost.

More generally, throughout the Joint Committee hearings of 1980–1, and the concurrent closed meetings of the Gang of Eight, the Charter's supporters, with their limited resources, paid negligible attention to the amending formula. Like most actors in the constitutional drama, with the possible exception of Prime Minister Trudeau and his key advisers, they showed little concern about the compatibility or otherwise of an amending formula and the Charter. Thus the potential conflict between the amending formula, which combined executive dominance with a version of federalism biased toward provincial governments, and the Charter, which showed a suspicion of governing élites and bias toward the pan-Canadian community, was ignored.

THE TWO MAJOR COMPONENTS of the Constitution Act of 1982 are based on very different visions of our country. They had different origins and followed separate routes into the constitution. Their coexistence in the same document reflects Ottawa's unyielding insistence that constitutional change include the nationalist thrust of a Charter and the equally unyielding insistence of the Gang of Eight that it include a provincialist, government-dominated amending formula.

The Charter reflected the new rights consciousness stimulated by both domestic and international factors. Its political purpose was to raise the status of citizens vis-à-vis governments and to strengthen the pan-Canadian community. The latter purpose explains why, among governments, the federal government aggressively sponsored the Charter as it emerged from and was transformed by a gruelling public committee process. The Charter linked numerous groups directly to the constitution for the first time. The constitutional culture it anticipated was non-deferential, somewhat mistrustful of governments, dubious about the centrality of federalism as a constitutional organizing principle, and, when further developed, might come to suggest that sovereignty did or should reside with the people. Thus, if the Charter had been entrenched while the formula for amendment was still unresolved, adoption of the existing amending formula would have been inconceivable.

The amending formula, by contrast, was a product of provincial governments. It emerged from an interprovincial arena and subsequently received acceptance in a closed first ministers' conference. Not surprising, it was a response to the provincial concerns that fashioned it, not to the proliferating constitutional lobby groups of women, ethnics, aboriginals, Charter advocates, and others, whose aggressive posture in public forums had a marked impact on the Charter. Further, the amending formula reflected a decentralist view of federalism that had developed in the 1960s and 1970s, as well as a tendency, documented by Robert Vipond, to fashion constitutional arguments in terms of the principles of federalism rather than in terms of constitutional origins or the intentions of the founders.[58] On the whole, this view of federalism stressed the provincial rather than the national dimension of Canadians' existence. Federalism became a rhetorical weapon to be employed against the national community and the federal government rather than a constitutional arrangement for the expression of the national and provincial dimensions of a people.

Conceptually, federalism verged on being equated with provincialism. In academic circles, the rubric "province-building" acquired high visibility for its drawing of attention to the neglected provincial counterpart of nation-building. Intrastate federalism, previously discussed, also stressed the provincial dimension of Canadian existence at a time when Canadian federalism was characterized by a centrifugal provincialism. It is perhaps not surprising that the "principles of federalism," as fashioned by governments least sympathetic to Ottawa and to the national community, should generate an amending formula expressive of "provincial governmentalism" or "governmental provincialism."

In the immediate aftermath of proclamation of the Constitution Act, the coexistence of the Charter and the amending formula, in spite of their distinctive origins and contrasting assumptions, was viewed as a somewhat abstract concern devoid of serious practical consequences. After all, they applied to different spheres and appealed to different constituencies. The amending formula, it might reasonably be thought, was of concern mainly to governments and was unlikely to be frequently applied. The Charter, by contrast, had been portrayed by the federal government as the chief component of a "People's Package," had attracted the bulk of the attention of the interest groups that appeared before the Special Joint Committee, and promised to become a significant resource in future judicial proceedings. None of this, however, suggested that the Charter's vision would seriously complicate the working of an amending formula dominated by governments.

The assumption that the Charter and the amending formula were on separate tracks that would not meet was given additional support by the knowledge that the citizens' groups that fought so vigorously for a more powerful Charter had displayed negligible enthusiasm for the federal amending proposals that would have enhanced the constitutional role of citizens. This absence of a positive response to the referendum idea analogous to the public support for the Charter suggested that the 1982 act represented an acceptable division of the constitutional spoils. It was the kind of outcome that one would expect from an intergovernmental political compromise in which the federal government had mobilized significant public support for its Charter project but had been unable to do the same for its proposed amending formula.

The amending formula and the Charter provide contrasting "answers" to the question: "To whom does the Constitution belong, governments or citizens?" This dichotomy might have mattered little if the amendment process were likely to rest unused on the constitutional shelf, while bureaucratic and political élites worked the federal system by less formal means. However, recent experience suggests that it is not easy to leave the constitution alone and get on with the task of governing. Proposals for formal constitutional change were a constant presence in the 1960s and 1970s. Further, the fact that the major perceived shortcoming of the 1982 act was the failure of Quebec's government to agree to its terms virtually guaranteed resort to the new amending procedure when an opportunity emerged to bring Quebec back into the constitutional family. The symbol of exclusion could be put right only by a symbolic act of inclusion, for which there was no alternative to formal amendment. Moreover, the task of enticing back an aggrieved Quebec government almost ensured, as turned out to be the case, that the resulting constitutional package ("Meech Lake") would be handled as a "text-book example of 'executive federalism'" or, more generally, of "'elite accommodation,'" with citizens as spectators.[59]

As the next chapter will argue, the attempt to overcome one major flaw in the 1982 compromise, exclusion of the government of Quebec, by employing the amending formula, which represented only one of the two competing visions enshrined in the constitution, made visible the other major flaw: ambivalence on the locus of sovereignty. The question that had not been previously asked, however, because of the two-track process in 1980–1 – about the practical compatibility between a government-dominated amending formula and a Charter that raises citizens' consciousness – could no longer be avoided.

The Constitution Act of 1982 left Canadians with two constitutional visions: one, organized around federalism concerns, is the preserve of governments; the second, focused on the Charter, stresses the citizen-state dimension from the perspective of the citizen. The governments' constitution is incomplete because the government of Quebec is not a willing party to its terms. The citizens' constitution is incomplete because its citizen beneficiaries have no automatic right of meaningful participation in amendment processes that might weaken their rights. The larger written constitution that contains them both is threatened with paralysis by the lack of agreement on the relative roles of governments and citizens in constitutional change. It is, accordingly, a task of the highest priority to find a modus vivendi between the Charter and the amending formula. The site of that resolution can be only in revised criteria, formal and/or informal, to govern the amending process in ways that do not assume that the Charter never happened. The issue, at base, is the locus of sovereignty.

With the benefit of hindsight, it now appears that post-1982 commentators, up to the appearance of Meech Lake, paid too much attention to the Charter, too little to the amending formula, and far too little to the circumstances in which their competing assumptions would clash. It is now apparent that citizens' rights carry with them an assumption of the right to participate in a serious way in the amendment of the framework in which those rights are contained. Thus defeat of an amending formula with a referendum option that would have been much more congruent with underlying Charter assumptions can now be seen to have left Canadians with a serious practical problem: who should participate, and in what ways, in formal constitutional amendment?

CONCLUSION

The Constitution Act, 1982, provided only a brief respite from constitutional introspection, although its achievements were considerable – including a new and comprehensive amending formula, a Charter of Rights binding on both orders of governments, and a resources clause beneficial to the provinces. Although there was a tendency at the time to denigrate the changes as limited or trivial, such a claim could not be credibly made in the late 1980s as Canadians digested the Charter. The significance of the Charter is not simply in its provision of a written code of rights and the availability of a judicial process to employ in their protection. More important, the Charter extended the reach of the constitution, in a pervasive yet discriminating fashion, deep into society. The constitution now matters to all the groups identified in the Charter, ranging from the specificity of individuals with mental or physical disabilities to the generality of "everyone" cited elsewhere.

The written constitution is no longer, as the BNA Act had been, a spare, spartan document that speaks mainly to governments; it is now a much more encompassing set of documents that reaches out to numerous new constituencies, such as women, official-language minorities, "multiculturalists," and others. Functionally, the constitution, as well as regulating the affairs of governments, now presides over the citizen-state relationship and is also the master instrument providing discriminating recognition to the multiple social categories of a heterogeneous modern society.

This extension of the constitution's reach is, indeed, so profound and pregnant with such societal significance that it will require Canadians to rethink what a constitution is. In the pre-Confederation decades, "constitution" meant responsible government to the politically active; subsequently, particularly in its written form, it came to mean federalism, especially the division of powers. The addition of the Charter further extends the embrace of the constitution.[60] These new layers do not displace what has gone before but must be incorporated in a new synthesis that will be the product of creative ingenuity.

The constitution bequeathed to Canadians by the additions of 1982 is not just a structural framework, a new container within which unchanged Canadians undertake their daily pursuits. Rather, it constitutes a pervasive environment of cues, incentives, and, in general, identity-shaping pressures.

The role of the constitution as an instrument of social management and rights protection does not sit easily with its traditional role of regulating the federal dimension of Canadian existence. A rapprochement has yet to be worked out between the constitutional role of the peoples and governments of Canada defined in federal terms ("the governments' constitution") and their newer role defined in terms of the citizen-state axis contained in the Charter (an emerging "citizens' constitution").

After the Constitution Act had been proclaimed, the captains and the queen departed, and the exploding fireworks in Ottawa and black armbands and flags at half-mast in Quebec made their symbolic statements of achievement and betrayal, the second stage of real constitutional change began. The constitutional word had to be made living flesh; the paper phrases had to be internalized; thousands of acts of discretion had to be informed by the new constitutional injunctions. The governors and the governed had to start learning to live the new constitutional order, not merely live in it, or under it, or off it. Further, Canadians could not respond to the major shortcoming of the Constitution Act – the Quebec government's opposition to its terms and the nationalist passions an inadequate response could inflame – as if the Charter did not exist.

We learn who we are and where we are both from our constitutional efforts that succeed, and from those that fail, and perhaps even more from those that are defined as failures by some and successes by others. That ambiguous legacy was the Constitution Act's gift to the first generation that had to assimilate its achievements while responding to its shortcomings. From this perspective, Meech Lake is another instructive development. Conceived as a high-risk effort to be stage-managed and brought to a quick conclusion by incumbent political and bureaucratic élites in the service of traditional concerns of federalism, Meech Lake ran into serious difficulty because its authors misunderstood the significance of the new constitutional currents set in motion by the Charter. Their appropriate sensitivity to the exclusion of Quebec was not matched by an equal sensitivity to the Charter's impact on Canada's constitutional culture.

CHAPTER FOUR

The Lessons of Meech Lake

IN THE EYE OF THE BEHOLDER

The lessons of a phenomenon such as Meech Lake will vary from one participant to another, by whether the outcome is seen as a success or a failure, by the time of judgment, and by whether the drawer of lessons is an involved actor or a more detached, perhaps scholarly observer. Thus to write of the lessons of Meech Lake does not imply that they will emerge automatically from a scientific research process that would unerringly lead all seekers to the same interpretation; nor is it to suggest that those in charge of our constitutional affairs would necessarily agree with the dossier of lessons in this chapter. One has to ask, "Lessons for whom?" Aboriginals, women, the Quebec government, and the Federal-Provincial Relations Office will not draw the same lessons from the constitutional experience called Meech Lake. In each case, lessons will be coloured by considerations of self-interest: how can *we* do better next time?

Further, for the participants, one way of doing better is to get others to agree with a version of lessons that will serve one's own interests in the next round. Indeed, in the practical game of constitutional politics, that is the first lesson. Here, the distinctions between lessons, abuse of history, disinformation, and the search for future advantage get badly blurred. Lessons are weapons. The search for lessons, therefore, is a highly politicized activity for constitutional activists. It overlaps with the pervasive political strategy of generating favourable interpretations of past events that will serve present purposes. The classic recent example was the signal achievement of successive Quebec governments in disseminating the thesis that their province had been betrayed in 1980–2, an interpretation that was plausible, but also clearly contestable.[1]

The lessons of Meech Lake cannot be divorced from the outcome. Early in the process, when Meech Lake could still be perceived as an irresistible juggernaut heading for implementation, Senator Lowell Murray, minister of state for federal-provincial relations, wrote an indulgent, somewhat complacent piece about the positive lessons to be drawn from the seemingly brilliant political engineering that lay behind the pending triumph. In particular, he favourably noted the narrow focus of the negotiations on five "limited and manageable" demands of Quebec, which avoided "paralyzing linkages with other constitutional issues."[2] Subsequently, both Murray and Prime Minister Mulroney reversed this analysis and attributed the difficulties that Meech Lake was experiencing to its necessarily limited focus on Quebec to rectify that province's exclusion by the Liberals in 1982. This regrettable if unavoidable concentration was now blamed for depriving the prime minister of "the benefit of flexibility that comes from a comprehensive negotiation."[3]

Had Meech Lake been saved at the last minute by an adroit symbolic concession from Robert Bourassa, by a decision by Elijah Harper and the Manitoba Indian chiefs not to filibuster in the Manitoba legislature, or by a successful cliff-hanging demonstration of Mulroney's vaunted powers of persuasion and conciliation, a different set of lessons would surely be drawn. Although the difference in background events and strategies between winning by a squeaker and losing by a squeaker may be minimal, the lens of triumph and the lens of defeat illuminate lessons that are worlds apart. With a victory, however narrow, the lessons are likely to be positive – what behaviour should we repeat to duplicate this success in future? With a defeat, they are negative – what behaviour should we avoid so that similar failures do not recur? The lessons of failure, accordingly, are likely to suggest major behavioural changes; success suggests more of the same.

However, even the basic concepts of victory and defeat fade and prove elusive when closely examined. Their application to a particular outcome varies from one set of constitutional actors to another and from one time period to another. In Quebec, Meech Lake will be seen as a clear defeat and will be interpreted through the prism of competing versions of Québécois nationalism. At a minimum, it will confirm for nationalists the tremendous difficulty of bending the constitution to satisfy Quebec's demands for some degree of distinctive constitutional recognition. For aboriginals, in contrast, passage of Meech Lake would have been a defeat, whereas its failure was seen as a victory for their blocking tactics.

The conditioning effect of time on evaluation is clear from a thought experiment. If, for example, Canada breaks up and the two successor states of Quebec-without-Canada and Canada-without-Quebec are separately successful and practise fruitful foreign relations with each other, Meech Lake may not appear a failure. It may come to be seen as a positive learning experience that confirmed the inevitability of separate futures for the two new peoples and states that emerged.

While these perplexities might appear to paralyse analysis and the drawing of conclusions, they are in fact the initial lesson to be extracted from Meech Lake – namely, that constitutional politics is never-ending and involves many actors, both public and private, with competing and evolving interests. Victories for some are likely to be defeats for others; positive lessons for some are negative ones for others. With the passage of time, reinterpretations occur, and victory and defeat and positive and negative lessons may change places. All the players separately remember, exploit, and draw their own lessons from the past as they reason purposefully about the future.

Thus the constitution has a scattered existence in a host of bureaucratic and private memories that select, distort, and forget in the service of particular aspirations. For participants, especially in times of conflict, constitutional visions and the search for understanding and lessons from the past are driven primarily by self-interest. The normative role and integrating capacity of the constitution writ large tend to fade from view. At such times, active players may forget to ask about who is to take care of the constitution or who will see it as a whole. Responsibility for asking and answering such questions devolves on others who are less involved. Thus a crucial lesson from Meech Lake for the scholarly community – or more gently phrased, a reminder – is that as constitutional conflict escalates, the scholarly role should not be entirely sacrificed on the altar of direct participation. Canadians will not suffer from a deficiency of partial, self-interested, short-term analysis if scholars resist getting in the trenches.

In view of the preceding, the considerable traffic between the academic community and direct participants should not obliterate the division of labour between them. Scholars should try to complement and supplement the partiality, passion, and immediacy of the participants by a lesser involvement in the fray, by employing a comprehensive perspective that encompasses as many of the players as is humanly possible, and by striving for the long view.

In this chapter, accordingly, I view Meech Lake as an opportunity for intensive learning about fundamental constitutional questions that are relevant to all the players. The lessons that follow are designed to help the reader understand the present state of the Canadian constitutional system and its degree of fit or dissonance with the society to which it applies. Specifically, of course, the focus is on the process of change – how did we in Meech Lake and how should we in future try to change direction by the process of formal amendment?

A BRIEF PLEA FOR
A CONSTITUTIONAL
ANTHROPOLOGY

The background for much of the analysis is the mountainous outpouring of commentaries, official statements, and presentations to various legislative committees that Meech Lake stimulated. I have immersed myself in particular in the proceedings of the public hearings in Parliament, Ontario, Manitoba, and New Brunswick until I thought I could hear the people talking. These hearings provide valuable insights into the emerging constitutional culture of Canada outside the world of politicians and administrators. They convince me that the scholar of the future must become an anthropologist of the many social worlds that now intersect with the constitution – particularly those that are somewhat removed from the official world views of the first ministers and their advisers, who sit at the apex of our political systems. The relevance of the constitution now extends beyond governments and the Canadian and provincial communities they serve to encompass women, aboriginals, visible minorities, the disabled, and a citizenry with rights. The modern Western nation-state is an arena for a profusion of particularistic forms of self-consciousness defined by sex, language, indigenousness, and so on that we do not understand "naturally" simply by cohabiting the same Canadian space.[4]

The secular tribalism of modernity can be encountered at home without undertaking distant expeditions. A crucial Meech Lake lesson, accordingly, is that a comprehensive constitutional understanding will no longer emerge from studying the élite worlds of executive federalism supplemented by the constrained constitutional discourse of the courtroom. Meech Lake makes clear that the constitution now has a social base. As a consequence, society now has a constitutional existence to a degree that previous generations would not have recognized. As the embrace between constitution and society tightens, those who work the former from the seats of power must not forget its interdependence with the latter. It follows that constitutional scholars must be students of society as well as of governments; their historic propensity to look upward to cabinets and courtrooms must be

broadened to encompass the citizenry and the constitutional linking
of state and society.

FROM A "LIVING" CONSTITUTION TO THE AGONY OF FORMAL CHANGE

Over the long haul, the Canadian experience of constitutional change
has been a success. The survival into the closing years of the twentieth
century of an order fashioned more than a century ago admits of no
other conclusion. Four provinces have grown to ten provinces and two
territories; the infant state of the 1860s has developed into the burgeoning state apparatus of the 1990s; struggling colonial societies
have evolved peacefully into a mature, independent people no longer
beholden to the former imperial mother country.

This evolution has been the product mainly of practical politicians
adjusting their inheritance to new demands. While formal change by
amendments has not been irrelevant, it has not been the central
instrument of change, partly because Canadians did not possess a
comprehensive domestic amendment procedure until 1982. The
demise of old practices and assumptions and the emergence of modified behaviour and beliefs have produced the flexibility that has
made the Canadian constitution a "living" arrangement.

The experience of recent decades has been less fortunate. Major
structural change has been sought by formal amendments. By infer-
ence, the extraconstitutional route has been deemed inadequate for
the objectives sought by some players. Cutting the imperial tie and
establishing a Canadian amending procedure, adding an entrenched
Charter of Rights, defining and entrenching aboriginal rights,
reforming the Senate to strengthen the role of the smaller provinces
in the central government, and elaborating a new status for Quebec
within or outside Canadian federalism have all been deeply divisive
issues. Their attempted resolution by formal amendment has produced more false starts and failures than successes.

Again and again, defeat has been snatched from the jaws of victory,
as with the 1964 Fulton-Favreau amending formula and the Victoria
Charter package of 1971, when the government of Quebec was
unwilling to proceed in the face of intense nationalist pressure at
home. When change has successfully been introduced, a recurrent
strategy has been to ignore or bypass objectors who disagree with
the direction of change. Thus Louis St Laurent refused to consult
the provinces when he proceeded to establish the Supreme Court as
the final court of appeal in 1949, "on the grounds that Duplessis

would never consent" to such a change.[5] Three decades later, until checked by the Supreme Court, Pierre Trudeau's Liberal government was clearly prepared to proceed with a unilateral request to Westminster for major constitutional change in the face of objections by eight provincial governments. Ultimately, a compromise was struck that excluded the Quebec government and led to bitter accusations of betrayal. In the shaping of this compromise, women and aboriginals found that the rights and guarantees they thought they had achieved were eliminated or modified. While these rights were largely restored after massive mobilization by both groups, they both shared a memory of attempted betrayal, or exclusion, similar to that of Quebec.

Meech Lake continues what threatens to became a tradition of excluding or bypassing those who, it was thought, could be safely ignored. Its working premise was that extragovernmental opposition to its means and ends could be rendered ineffectual and be overridden if first ministers would simply stick together and employ party discipline to rush the appropriate resolutions through submissive legislatures. Meech Lake itself was preceded by four constitutional conferences that failed to define the rights of aboriginal peoples and, in particular, failed to entrench their right of self-government. Aboriginal leaders left the conference table feeling embittered, cheated, and convinced that they had not been taken seriously.

Accordingly, the scholar is advised to become comfortable with an almost operatic language of the emotions, in which betrayal, treachery, dishonour, deception, distrust, and bad faith are liberally sprinkled through the accusing language of the losers. Indeed, from one perspective, the constitutional choice reduces to those who are in control deciding who should be left out. Recently, women, aboriginals and the government of Quebec have been prominent candidates – the former two groups because their claims outrun their influence and the latter because after the referendum Quebec's good faith was doubted by some of the other governments and Ottawa held a rival version of relations between Quebec and Canada and between French and English. Unfortunately, such victories – constructed on an edifice of losers, like the Constitution Act of 1982 and Meech Lake, had it passed – would have made Canada the modern-day epitome of a Pyrrhic victory. The book title *And No One Cheered*[6] applied to the 1982 act could equally have served for a successful Meech Lake outcome in 1990, although it might have been rejected as too positive.

Major formal constitutional change is a perilous enterprise. There are now many more players than formerly. Their demands appear to be increasingly incompatible. Potential losers multiply. The Charter has generated new orientations to the constitution that clash with the federalist bias that remains natural to governments. The constitution we have inherited that was formerly hallowed by tradition now appears to many to be simply old and decrepit. Finally, of course, since a comprehensive amending formula was added in 1982, Canadians are now on their own, with no one to blame but themselves. Meech Lake, therefore, should be treated as a valuable scholarly resource from which worthwhile lessons, debatable though they may be, can be extracted to improve our future performance. Formal constitutional change is the most demanding and significant political activity available to a free people. Canadians do it badly. A search for the big lessons of Meech Lake may help us to do better in future.

THE AMENDING PROCESS AND THE FAILURE OF EXECUTIVE FEDERALISM

The staggering rebuff of executive federalism in constitutional matters implicit in the failure of Meech Lake is perhaps its most basic lesson. An agreement originally supported by all eleven governments could not be carried through to completion. The enterprise was noble in its aspiration to return Quebec to the constitutional family and politically shrewd in rounding up support from all provincial governments by offering them the same package received by Quebec, except for the "distinct society" provision. Also, both Liberal and New Democratic federal opposition parties initially supported the package for a mixture of patriotic reasons and self-interested hopes for electoral success in Quebec.

The agreeing governments based their leading role in this initiative on their habitual dominance of the intergovernmental arena of executive federalism where the agreement was worked out and on the dominant role of political executives in the eleven systems of responsible government where legislative approval by resolution was required. The propriety of their leadership was also sustained by their definition of the issue – to bring Quebec back into the family of Canadian federalism was obviously an issue for governments to handle. Further, the amending formula they applied had been drafted by provincial governments to ensure government domination of the process and to thwart Trudeau's rival proposals, which would have given a referendum role to the electorate.[7] In the circumstances, the governments' assumptions that they both did and should run the Meech Lake show were not surprising.

In the immediate aftermath of the Langevin Block agreement clothing the Meech Lake Accord in appropriate legal language, there was no reason to doubt their confidence. The belief that Meech Lake was destined for quick and easy ratification was almost ubiquitous. The federal government believed so. Lowell Murray subsequently attributed the absence of a federal public relations campaign on behalf of the accord to the belief that it would be implemented within a year.[8] Prime Minister Mulroney was brutally explicit in his reiterated assertions that the premiers had agreed to a deal, their word was their bond, and they were expected to deliver on their commitment.[9] It followed that educating and involving the public was unnecessary and dysfunctional. Hence the attempt was made to run Meech Lake almost as a military operation – closed meetings, decisive action, the premature victory announcement, and an indication that a few mopping-up operations in legislatures remained to be completed.[10] Thus the lavish attention devoted to ensuring that all first ministers were on side was not duplicated for the public at large or for the many groups with constitutional interests derived from the Charter and aboriginal clauses. Legislative approval was considered little more than a formality, almost an afterthought. This grievous miscalculation was graphically revealed in the flattering apologia for the Meech Lake process delivered by Lowell Murray in February 1988.[11] He implicitly equated the amending process with the intergovernmental agreement that was only its first stage and thus intimated that Meech Lake was in the bag at a time when it was heading into deep trouble.

What went wrong? Explanations are to be found in the interaction between the rules governing this major effort at constitutional change and a society for which Meech Lake's definition of what Canada was about was no longer convincing. In retrospect, the governments that orchestrated Meech Lake seriously misunderstood the complex rules governing constitutional change and were profoundly out of touch with basic changes in the constitutional culture of Canadians, especially outside Quebec, triggered mainly by the Charter.

The first ministers failed to grasp the potential significance of the requirement for legislative ratification and of the three-year period within which it could take place in the eleven jurisdictions. Accordingly, they collapsed a two-stage process – getting the agreement of first ministers and then proceeding to a second and discrete stage of legislative approval – into one stage, with legislative approval flowing expeditiously and automatically from the prior agreement of the governments whose concerns had been met. It logically followed that the agreement was relatively indifferent to the potential concerns of the various social interests – women, aboriginal Canadians, northerners, devotees of the Charter – who thought that their concerns were damaged by the accord and who emerged in the second stage.

The indifference of governments to these many worlds was facilitated by several characteristics of the early accord process. The secrecy of the preliminary negotiations and the rapid consummation of the initial agreement insulated first ministers from public opinion by depriving it of a focus and of time to crystallize before the accord was declared final and unalterable.

This insulation was aggravated by the requirement of unanimity that the first ministers imposed on the package, though not all elements needed approval of Ottawa and the ten provinces under the Constitution Act, 1982. Unanimity of governments, especially when combined with the official support of all three parties in the House of Commons, deprived the public of alternative, opposing views to challenge the political hegemony of the accord's government supporters. Initially, also, the unanimity was intimidating to potential opponents, who experienced an intellectual and political loneliness that easily led to doubts about the validity as well as the realism of their opposition. Ultimately, however, unanimity ill-served the élites that had appeared to benefit from it, for it contributed to their cocoon-like ignorance of the public opinion that would later be their undoing.

The development of opposition to the accord was facilitated by several of the formal rules of the amending process. The new provision placed in the Constitution Act, 1982, requiring resolutions by legislatures transformed the politics of the amending process. Consequently, since 1982, consummation of a first ministers' agreement waits on legislative ratification by the most dilatory among the necessary number of governments. The legislative process ensured political visibility to the proposed amendments, ranging from minuscule in British Columbia to substantial in Ontario, Manitoba, New Brunswick, and Parliament, where reasonable hearings processes were undertaken.[12] The Liberal-dominated Senate, although it had only a suspensive veto of 180 days, displayed great ingenuity in providing opponents of the accord with a variety of platforms.[13]

When the process drags out, as it did in Meech Lake, the three-year period for ratification gave time for opposition to develop, for governments to be defeated and replaced by new governments not party to the initial agreement (as in Manitoba, New Brunswick, and Newfoundland), for two of the latter to hold public hearings that focused opposition to the accord, for the third to revoke the supporting resolution passed by a previous legislature (Newfoundland),

and for other governments to waver under the impact of hostile public opinion from the official support they had previously offered and confirmed by legislative action (British Columbia).

These developments could have been anticipated, as being in the nature of things. A typical three-year period over the past decade and a half has featured nine federal or provincial elections, three of which result in changes of government.[14] The likelihood that such changes will weaken support for a pending constitutional agreement is high, given the tendency of opposition parties to oppose the government in systems of adversarial politics, especially on issues where public support for the government's position is weak or fragile.

Even if the opposition parties are on side, their commitment is less than that of the governments that are parties to an agreement. A straightforward political logic virtually ensures that a unanimous agreement of governments is unlikely to be maintained among the opposition parties that seek to displace them, assuming enough time for the initial hegemony of supporting opinion to be broken. The interaction between eleven systems of parliamentary government and an initial constitutional consensus of executive federalism induces opposition parties to play the role of spoilers. Given the ratio of ten provincial to one federal government, the successful elected spoiler is most likely to be provincial.

By the time of the demise of Meech Lake, opposition to it was led by three newly elected provincial governments that had replaced incumbent Meech Lake supporters; the four western NDP leaders had come out against the accord,[15] as had the four western Liberal leaders.[16] According to one newspaper account, as the accord entered its third year, every provincial Liberal leader, except the three premiers who helped negotiate it, was opposed.[17] Nova Scotia's Liberal leader Vince MacLean shared the views of Manitoba Liberal leader Sharon Carstairs and promised to try and renegotiate the agreement if elected.[18] Preston Manning's western-based Reform Party was also strongly opposed to Meech Lake[19] and threatened to run candidates in the next BC provincial election if the Social Credit government did not take strong action against the accord.[20]

In sum, the requirement of legislative approval provides access to the public in two ways: first, by the compulsory debates and optional hearings it generates and, second, by the delay it is likely to occasion, thus facilitating changes of governments, following elections. The elections in Manitoba, New Brunswick, and Newfoundland dramatically opened up the process by providing leadership to the opponents of Meech Lake. Remarkably, the premiers of these three provinces became national figures, partly because they gave voice to a strong central-government pan-Canadian vision that was popular in English Canada and was not eloquently supported by any of the three federal parties. Further, the 1988 federal election, in which the Conservatives won 60 of 75 seats from Quebec, gravely weakened federal Liberal and NDP support for the accord, much of which had been based on the hopes of electoral success in Quebec. Finally, Liberal and NDP leadership campaigns became additional vehicles for pervasive anti–Meech Lake sentiments among rank-and-file party members.

Thus, in Meech Lake the three-year period and required legislative ratification undermined the élite dominance of supporting governments that characterized the onset of the process. If ratification is delayed, the initial consensus is likely to erode. Delay holds out the possibility that an election will become a vehicle to overturn a consensus incompletely ratified by legislatures. Further, when either constitutional requirement or adopted political practice dictates unanimity, the defection of a single province will stall the process and stimulate the politics of opposition throughout the system.[21]

The requirement for legislative ratification also weakens governments' capacity to show flexibility in the face of criticism and thus salvage an accord by modifying its details. Once the agreement has been struck, drafted in legislative language, and passed by one or more governments, any subsequent change requires a return to the legislature for new approval. In contrast, in the 1981–2 situation, "a single telephone call between governments would suffice to achieve agreement on amendments," given the absence of a formal amending formula and the more limited requirement of a Joint Address of the Senate and the House of Commons to Westminster.[22] For the governments involved, return to the legislature for new approval can be a very high-risk venture. Thus even limited public pressure produced a few significant changes between the initial Meech Lake agreement and the final legal document to emerge from the Langevin Block meetings; yet massive pressure over three years produced no changes after the legal text was rapidly confirmed as definitive by Quebec's legislative ratification three weeks later. The rise and fall of sensitivity are rule-determined.[23]

Logically, therefore, given the rules in place, the completion of a Meech Lake–type amending process admits of only two possible strategies for successful passage. One might conclude that a similar enterprise in future should be conducted even more brutally and expeditiously as a hit-and-run affair of governments before the messy pluralist politics of Canadian democracy can be stirred into action.

Such an approach might even be dressed in the garments of constitutional necessity, or reason of state, the argument being that on this particular occasion governments must act outside the bounds of normally acceptable behaviour because the survival of the state is in the balance. There were hints of this in the rationales behind Prime Minister Trudeau's threat to act unilaterally in 1980–1 and in some of the belated attempts to justify the Meech Lake process.

Evidently, the kind of statist tradition required to justify such action is only weakly developed in Canada. Further, its application to a collective act of at least eight or up to eleven governments, depending on the applicable amending formula, would likely founder on the difficulty of co-ordinating the conduct of so many autonomous actors. With or without a reason-of-state rationale, success depends on the speed of the operation. Meech Lake indicates that delay undermines the initial élite consensus and the capacity of the initiating élite to monopolize the debate.

The alternative to an attempted collective unilateralism of governments is to accept the reality of both stages of the process. This can be done in several ways. A limited modification of Meech Lake practice would require governments to construct their initial intergovernmental agreement in a way that is sensitive to the concerns of the interests that will appear in stage 2. Obviously, this will produce a different package of proposals, one that blends the concerns of governments and those of the groups whose interests are significantly involved in the area under discussion.

An even looser process would involve some combination of preliminary hearings followed by a tentative intergovernmental agreement and then a follow-up round of further hearings before governments come to a final agreement on the package to be put before their legislatures. This will not be an easy process to work. The evidence of both Meech Lake and 1980–2 is that the issues, concerns, and perspectives shift dramatically as discussion moves from the intergovernmental arena to the public world of hearings and private interests. As Robert Campbell notes, the move from the former to the latter in Meech Lake was from a closed world of deals dominated by provincial governments' concerns to a public arena, where such concerns were all but displaced by a "bewildering and eclectic array of issues: women's rights, multiculturalism, national social programs, native rights, the status of the territories, language issues, the efficacy of the federal government, and so on."[24] When this babble of voices breaks through, is heard, and responded to, as in the Report of the Charest Committee with its twenty-three recommendations,[25] the outraged reaction of those who see the world in terms of governments, or federalism, or Quebec/Canada indicates that bridging the citizen-government gap will be extraordinarily challenging.[26]

The gap between the constitutional concerns of governments and those of citizen groups reflects the different worlds in which they live. It is, however, also a product of a process of constitutional change that does little to bring these worlds together and to generate understanding of and empathy for the concerns of each by the other. When the amending process is operated as a self-interested juggernaut of governments attempting to bulldoze its way over the often competing concerns of citizens, who are given only sporadic opportunities to speak and negligible opportunity to be heard, the inevitable result is a conflict of competing versions of calculating self-interest. This can be avoided only by an extension of the principle of what J.A. Corry pleaded for in relations among governments – a constitutional morality that is ever sensitive to the concerns of other governments, all of whom cohabit a system that is expected to endure.[27] That constitutional morality must now embrace all the actors who have stakes in the constitutional order. It requires reciprocal sensitivity and a buildup of trust in both directions as the worlds of governments and citizens are brought closer together in the process of constitutional change. The traditional argument that responsible, elected governments can be trusted to represent the interests of a heterogeneous citizen body in constitutional matters is no longer believed.

For governments, the requisite changes in the first instance are those of attitude and ideas that involve a more rounded perspective on the constitution. These, however, will require organizational backup. One overlooked factor in the Meech Lake fiasco is that the leading constitutional advisers of governments in the Federal-Provincial Relations Office and its provincial counterparts are organizationally conditioned to see the constitutional world from a too limited and now inadequate federalist perspective.

THE NEW CONSTITUTIONAL CULTURE

The incentives to opposition provided by the rules that governed the Meech Lake process would have been much less significant had there either been a pervasive willingness to trust élites to manage our constitutional affairs or had the accord simply constitutionalized a prevailing consensus about the desirable direction of change. Neither of these applied, because the accord clashed with the developing ethnic demography of Canada and the surprisingly strong English-

Canadian allegiance to the Charter. Charter-derived assumptions about participation also greatly stimulated hostility to the Meech Lake process.

The significance of ethnicity and rights reflected the expanded function of the constitution in the era of the Charter. The constitution is no longer just an affair of governments; its contents are no longer confined to the traditional ordering principles of federalism and parliamentary government; and hence the constitutional identities of Canadians are no longer restricted to their membership in Canadian and provincial communities, supplemented by a surviving emotional link with the monarchy for dwindling numbers.

The constitution now draws Canadians directly into the constitutional order via the Charter. The latter's fundamental political tendency is to elevate the status of citizens vis-à-vis governments and thus reduce deference. The traditional electoral check on incompetence and arrogance is now supplemented by a rights-based check that operates not only through the courts but also as a general frame of reference through which the interactions of citizens and authorities are monitored.

The Ethnic Dimension

The contemporary constitution addresses the ethnic heterogeneity of Canadian society. The written constitution has always been sensitive to ethnicity, with a preamble referring to a "Constitution similar in Principle to that of the United Kingdom," allocation of legislative authority over "Indians, and Lands reserved for the Indians" to the federal government (section 91[24]), and indirectly in the limited French-and-English-language requirements of section 133. Federalism itself was, among other things, dictated by the necessity of giving Quebec's francophone majority a significant sphere of jurisdictional autonomy free of the constraints provided by the English-speaking majority in Parliament.

This relatively stable ethnic accommodation broke down under the multiple impact of Québécois nationalism which sought a larger sphere of autonomy, politicization of the aboriginal people, fears of Europeans who were neither British nor French that they would lose status if the French and English "founding" peoples tightened their grip on the official definition of Canada, and emerging visible minorities that put race relations on the Canadian public agenda.

The decline of the historic ethnic consensus triggered two ethnic policy agendas. The first, which lay behind the Royal Commission on Bilingualism and Biculturalism of the late 1960s and the host of task forces and parliamentary inquiries devoted to national unity that followed, sought more fruitful coexistence between the French and English communities. This dualist agenda was, from Quebec's perspective, federalist: driven by the insistent pressures of successive Quebec governments for enhanced jurisdictional powers and for a provincial language regime that recognized and supported the pre-eminence of the French language. Quebec, where the majority of francophones live and constitute a provincial majority has always been the largest part of an answer to the question of how French and English could cohabit the same polity and territory without frustrating each other's objectives. Admittedly, the federal government under Trudeau consistently supported a language policy based on the personality principle rather than the territorial principle. The latter would have been more compatible with federalism by officially recognizing French-language dominance in Quebec and anglophone dominance elsewhere, except for of a bilingual belt in Ontario and the strong Acadian presence in New Brunswick. However, Trudeau's own academic writings underline his strong belief in federalism as the most functional arrangement for the flourishing of Quebec and French Canada.[28]

The second ethnic agenda, broader and more diffuse, went beyond French-English relations to encompass aboriginal peoples, visible minorities, and multicultural Canadians. The task here was to evolve an acceptable definition of Canada that symbolically included the growing ethnic heterogeneity of a people whose Britishness and Frenchness were of diminishing significance[29] and to grapple with the practical problems of ethnic and racial pluralism, especially in the major metropolitan centres of Vancouver, Toronto, and Montreal. This new agenda responded to a shifting ethnic demography. The British component of the population, which dropped from about 60 per cent at Confederation, to below 50 per cent in 1940, will soon be below 40 per cent. The French-origin population fell below 30 per cent in the early 1960s and is now nearing 25 per cent. By 1981, the "other" component had passed French and now constitutes more than one-third of the population. It is growing rapidly and by the turn of the century is projected to surpass 40 per cent of the population. Further, within the category "other," visible minorities will approach 10 per cent of the population early in the twenty-first century, not counting aboriginals.[30] Constitutional recognition of and self-government for aboriginal (especially status Indian) Canadians, along with measures to alleviate their Third World socioeconomic conditions, were a parallel and complex ethnic agenda.

With the possible exception of an Inuit-dominated province of Nunavut in northern Canada, the appropriate legislative and constitutional policy response to these indigenous, ethnic, and racial issues could not be transformed into an issue of federalism, as was true of much of the French-English search for an accommodation. The Canadian Bill of Rights; the evolution of the policy of multiculturalism, culminating in section 27 of the Charter; the halting steps to work out an acceptable status for aboriginal peoples; a proliferation of human rights commissions; and the Charter itself were prominent components of the state's response to ethnic issues outside the French-English dimension.

Meech Lake was the setting for a confrontation between these old and new ethnic agendas. The Meech Lake attempt to respond to the traditional French-English dualist dimensions of Canadian society and history clashed with newer ethnic concerns. A linked pair of Meech Lake lessons, therefore, is that the French-English constitutional issue can no longer be separated from other ethnic agendas and that federalism is a response to only one, even if the most state-threatening, of the tensions arising from new and old ethnic pluralism.

The constitutional hegemony of British and French "charter" groups and "founding" peoples is eroding, challenged by the shifting demography and politicization of ethnicity. Founding status is repudiated by aboriginal First Nations, which assert their own priority, while the citizens who make up multicultural and multiracial Canada are typically hostile to dualist conceptions of the country. The widespread tendency for the spokespersons for those Canadians who lack "founding" status to criticize Meech Lake for being backward-looking, for defining yesterday's rather than tomorrow's Canada, provides powerful testimony that a dualist definition of Canada is on the defensive. As William Thorsell recently and validly observed, the "traditional vision of the country, [and one that Meech Lake sought to bolster] – that of two founding peoples (chronically ignoring aboriginals) – is simply not experienced by the great majority of Canadians in their daily lives."[31] Hence the ubiquitous claim from organizations speaking for those non-"founding" Canadians that multiculturalism should have been given constitutional recognition in the accord as a fundamental characteristic along with linguistic duality.[32]

A similar challenge comes from aboriginal peoples, whose spokespersons invariably insist that they be recognized as distinct societies and included as one of Canada's fundamental characteristics. Their constitutional demands have a distinctive characteristic derived from the aboriginal claim to be First Nations and resulting resistance to incorporation in the multicultural category. Status Indians specifically and aboriginals generally have recognitions and rights scattered through the constitution that encourage them to see themselves as a distinctive constitutional category based on their indigenous status. The combination of growing numbers, experienced leadership, and political and constitutional consciousness ensures them of a distinct if ambiguous place in the constitutional order, the details of which remain to be worked out. The lesson of Meech Lake is clearly that their disruptive capacity, if nothing else, is sufficiently well developed that to exclude or ignore them is to risk paying a high price.

An ethnic constitutional discourse dominated by French-English relations, which could be translated into a federalism discourse by Quebec's political power, has lost ground. The ethnicity of the new non-aboriginal, multicultural, and multiracial Canada largely concentrated in metropolitan centres cannot be "managed" by federalism. Federalism can contribute to interethnic harmony or civility only when the ethnic groups in question are territorially concentrated and thus capable of escaping from each other by exercising limited powers of self-government in provinces or states. For the emergent ethnicity of metropolitan Canada, federalism provides no solution. The new ethnicity is characterized by multiple backgrounds, minority status within all political jurisdictions, and, for visible minorities, memories of past and fears of future discrimination. Whether the country survives in its present form or not, Canadians are becoming a new people for whom the past of Wolfe and Montcalm is truly another country and for whom federalism has declined in instrumental value.

French and English Canadians are defined increasingly by language, as French- and English-speaking Canadians. Both groups are undergoing profound internal transformations as they become ethnically and racially heterogeneous. Anglophone Canada is no longer British but has become a bewildering, eclectic ethnic smorgasbord in which the traditional diversity of the prairies is supplemented by an immigration-driven diversity, especially in Toronto and Vancouver. Precisely the same phenomenon is occurring in Quebec, albeit at a slower rate, except for Montreal. Quebec's French-speaking majority, which historically thought of itself as a common-descent group whose numbers were sustained by a high birthrate, is now becoming a multi-origin community that is multicultural and multiracial. For both groups, francophones in Quebec and anglophones throughout Canada, identity can no longer be derived from a history of the triumphs and defeats of the "race" nor from a historically shared ethnicity but must come rather from some combination of belonging to a linguistic community and also to provincial and Canadian territorial communities of citizenship.

The Meech Lake process has given Canadians a rapid learning experience in who they are that would have occurred much more slowly had our recent past been one of halcyon constitutional stability. Meech Lake has underlined the existence of aboriginal peoples who will not cede priority of founding status to French and English latecomers. Meech Lake has also laid bare the constitutional tension between a historic view of Canada defined in terms of relations between French and English, which remains natural to practitioners of executive federalism, and an emerging view outside the aboriginal communities which is hostile to making invidious distinctions between early arrivals and newcomers. This latter view, of course, has been embedded in prairie political culture almost from the beginning – belief in ethnic pluralism and rejection of special treatment for any one ethnic group. Contemporary conditions should facilitate its diffusion.

The self-interest of non-founding peoples whose numbers are fed by immigration suggests either an unhyphenated Canadianism that washes out differences based on time of arrival or a comprehensive multiculturalism that includes French and English. In either case, the pressure of the new ethnicity on the constitution of the future, aboriginals excepted, will be hostile to a pecking order based on time alone. Given the ethnic demographic projections cited previously, that pressure will not easily be marginalized. Given the reality of the French fact in Canada, sustained by the political power of the second most populous province, neither will it be easily accommodated.

The French fact in Quebec, however, is decreasingly sustained by a common culture, religion, or origin, and it shares its provincial territory with others – the English-speaking minority, allophones, and aboriginal peoples, whose non-aboriginal language is typically English. Thus francophone Québécois, like anglophones in the rest of Canada, coexist with linguistic others on their territory, confront a competing nationalism from aboriginal people, and experience a growing pluralism within their own linguistic community. The contemporary descendants of the early settlers are in effect only part, albeit the largest, of the French-language community, which in turn is only part, again the largest, of the Quebec fact. These are inescapable realities for all the citizens of Quebec and for the nationalism of its francophone majority.

The transition from a historic people to a community of language speakers is more advanced in English Canada than in Quebec's francophone majority, but the direction of change is similar and irresistible in both cases. Communities united by language may be riven by ethnic, racial, and religious struggles. They lack the identity and cohesion that comes from common ancestry and a historic sense of peoplehood. Their constitutional clout and legitimacy are weaker.

Meech Lake, therefore, drives home the valuable if painful lesson that the role of the constitution in managing and reflecting Canadian ethnicity is much more complex and difficult than we had believed. An appropriate constitutional response must speak to the ethnic and indigenous pluralism of the future, which increasingly constitutes the social fabric of both linguistic communities, and to the aboriginal realities that have and will retain some degree of special treatment.

Aboriginals, the Charter, and Constitutional Culture

A central message, one neither welcomed nor anticipated by Meech Lake strategists, is that the Charter has taken root, especially in English Canada, and the process of constitutional change must adapt to this new situation. It must also adapt to aboriginal involvement, strengthened by the Constitution Act, 1982.

A recurrent theme of interveners in the public hearings about Meech Lake was to protect the Charter against "the assault ... contained in the Meech Lake proposals."[33] Any weakening of its relative constitutional status, or apparent indifference to its potent symbolism, was construed as an attack on the constituencies that attach themselves to it. The hearings confirmed that the Charter taps powerful sentiments of citizens' identification. It is the third pillar of a constitutional order hitherto characterized by the primacy of parliamentary government and federalism. New Brunswick's Select Committee described the Charter as the "most important [of all the constitutional acts] for individual Canadians" and recommended including it in the accord as a fundamental characteristic of Canada.[34] Particularly in English Canada, the political purposes of the Charter – giving citizens a stake in the constitutional order and stimulating their identification with a pan-Canadian community of rights-bearers – have been resoundingly met, especially in the élites of organizations with Charter sympathies.

Clauses in the Charter and on aboriginal constitutional concerns are focal points for the constitutional identities of the clientele they encompass. For women, the sex-equality clause (section 28) is seen as a triumphant constitutional possession won against heavy odds by the efforts of women activists in the struggles that produced the Charter. To weaken section 28 – to filter its potency through the distinct society interpretive clause of the accord or to provide protection against such interpretation to clauses of concern to aboriginals and "multiculturals" (as section 16 of the accord did), but not to section 28 – was resisted as diminishing the status of women in the constitution and in Canadian society. In this way, the public ratification process became a vehicle for women to protect what was formerly won and now appeared threatened.

For aboriginal Canadians, section 25 of the Charter, section 35 of the Constitution Act, 1982, and section 91(24) of the BNA Act – "Indians, and Lands reserved for the Indians" – perform a function analogous to that of section 28 for women. Thus, although aboriginals got these clauses exempted from the distinct society clause, Meech Lake transmitted other negative messages about their position in Canadian society. Unlike French-speakers and English-speakers, they were not described as constituting "a fundamental characteristic of Canada," and unlike Quebec they were not to be constitutionally recognized as one (or more) distinct societies within Canada. Thus, from their perspective, they lost constitutional ground in the accord. The accord's message was that, although they might be constitutional players, they were only marginally so, and they played with a weak hand. The message, however, was effectively repudiated by the contribution of Elijah Harper and the Manitoba Assembly of Chiefs to blocking passage of the accord in Manitoba.

Involvement in Meech Lake by women and aboriginals was duplicated by official language minorities, which feared that the accord would weaken educational rights of section 23 of the Charter;[35] by the ethnic groups that fought the multicultural battle on behalf of section 27; by groups, including the disabled and visible minorities, that were concerned that the accord might weaken the equality rights in section 15; and more generally by those who supported the Charter as such, as an enhancement of citizens' rights and status. In this way, the Charter structured the constitutional debate by generating organizations devoted to its defence, often with agendas devoted to protection or enhancement of specific clauses.

The evidence from Meech Lake confirms what political logic would suggest: that giving Canadians constitutional rights elicits a political response when those rights appear to be challenged or ignored. The Charter and aboriginal clauses provide both the incentives and the self-confidence to participate in constitutional affairs. Those who identify with the Charter in general, with clauses in it, or with the aboriginal sections of the constitution no longer see themselves as only the audience to the real, parliamentary players. On the contrary, they were deeply offended by the Meech Lake process, which sought to deprive them of anything more than ritual input. The Charter and the aboriginal clauses, therefore, have helped to create an enlarged cast of actors outside government who are nervously concerned about how constitutional changes may affect "their" Charter or "their" aboriginal clauses or aspirations.

The public hearings over Meech Lake displayed a remarkably truculent attitude by individual citizens, interest group leaders, academics, and others toward the first ministers and their advisers for their false assumption that the constitution was theirs to amend as they saw fit. It is impossible to read this evidence without concluding that the Charter has, by changing citizens' identities and expectations, eroded the legitimacy of executive federalism, unconstrained by citizen input, as a vehicle for formal constitutional change. The reports from public hearings, responding to interveners, were highly critical of the secrecy and élitism of the process and the absence of flexibility once the official version of the accord had been made public.[36]

These new players, inspired mainly by the Charter, are hostile to government monopolization of the amending process. They see public participation as an issue no longer of procedural choice but rather of obligatory constitutional morality. For the interveners before Ontario's Select Committee, the process of how and by whom the accord was fashioned was "a theme more widely and frequently addressed ... than any substantive matter."[37] The procedures of executive federalism, according to Ontario's attorney-general, may be "being overtaken by rapidly-evolving opinions about citizen participation in public policy making."[38] The members of the Manitoba Task Force on Meech Lake "were struck by the impression that the presenters felt a sense of being cheated, misled, and betrayed ... [and] realized the extent to which the process ... undercut the legitimacy of the Accord."[39]

The antipathy to executive federalism is not confined to a narrow stratum of frustrated interest group leaders with delusions of constitutional grandeur but is shared at least superficially at the mass citizen level. A poll taken after the collapse of the Meech Lake Accord indicated that two out of three Quebecers, and an even higher ratio in the rest of Canada, believed that "changes to the constitution should only be decided by the people voting directly in a referendum."[40] At least in constitutional matters, therefore, Charles Taylor's thesis – that the rights orientation stimulated by the Charter weakens the participatory impulse – is invalid.[41] Indeed, the reverse is true, as the psychological fallout from the Charter challenges executive dominance of the constitutional order.

Consequently, Meech Lake lays bare a serious contradiction at the heart of the constitutional order that focuses on the amending formula. The conflict over the substance and process of Meech Lake indicates that the compromise of 1982 is unstable not only because Quebec's government was not party to it but also because of the tension between governments' view of the constitution, focusing on federalism, and the citizens' view, focusing on the Charter and on aboriginal clauses. Whether knowingly or inadvertently, the organizers of Meech Lake tried and failed to repudiate the social forces pressing for a more public and participatory process of constitutional change.[42]

The Charter and aboriginal clauses do not sit in the constitution as discrete self-contained entities impervious to their surroundings. Rather, their behaviour is imperialistic, as their solicitous clientele seeks to extend their influence into other arenas, such as the amending formula. The possessors of Charter (or aboriginal) rights, clauses, constitutional niches, and identities view themselves not as supplicants begging to be noticed but rather as legitimate participants entitled to try and advance their interests. The largest single category of interveners in public hearings from English Canada came from Charter constituencies, followed by an impressive array of spokespersons for aboriginal concerns. Both original supporters of the Charter, such as Jean Chrétien, and early opponents, such as Allan Blakeney, agree that the Charter has transformed the politics of constitutional reform by giving Canadians an explicit stake in the constitution – what Blakeney called a "possessor interest."[43]

The Charter and aboriginal clauses challenge not only governments' dominance of the amending formula but also the concomitant priority given to the national and provincial cleavages structured by federalism. In particular, the Charter dilutes sympathy for provincialism among English Canadians. In the Meech Lake contest, between a province-strengthening document and the Charter, the residents of Ontario, Manitoba, and New Brunswick, where extensive hearings were held, overwhelmingly supported the Charter and opposed an accord that strengthened the political power and jurisdiction of their province.

The concerns of citizens' groups brought into the constitution by the Charter and aboriginal clauses go beyond the narrowly instrumental to encompass issues of personal identity, symbolic considerations, and one's relative place in the constitutional status hierarchy. The differences that shape their constitutional claims are defined by

sex, ethnicity, indigenousness, race, disabilities, and so on, all of
which now have a constitutional dimension. It is therefore not surprising that these groups, defined non-territorially,[44] do not see themselves as adequately represented in closed sessions by governments
whose natural bent is to defend territory, strengthen jurisdiction,
and, as in Meech Lake, repair a malfunctioning federalism.

The Charter, Political Unity, and Quebec

The Charter was conceived for nation-building purposes as well as
an instrument of rights protection.[45] At the most general level, it was
hoped that as Canadians assimilated their new status as holders of
enforceable rights into their self-conceptions as citizens, they would
be encouraged to think of themselves in pan-Canadian terms. A
modified and strengthened country-wide identity would, relatively,
weaken provincial senses of community and identity. At this level, the
Charter was an attack on the conception of Canada as a community
of communities which flourished in the province-building 1960s and
1970s. For Pierre Trudeau, believing with Ernest Renan that a nation
is a "plebiscite of every day," the Charter was intended to increase the
probability that the never-ending plebiscite on Canadian togetherness
would receive a "yes" answer.

A vital political component of the Charter was to prevent the
coincidence of linguistic and provincial boundaries, for which the
essential tool was section 23, the clause on minority-language educational rights. Section 23 gave a right, in specified circumstances,
for children to be educated in the official minority language of their
parents – French outside Quebec and English inside Quebec. This
policy was clearly based on a view of the constitution as an instrument
of Canadianism, requiring provincial governments to provide minority-language educational services that could not be entrusted to the
normal working of provincial majoritarian democracy. The assumption was that if a conception of French Canada extending beyond
Quebec could be kept alive by constitutional stimulation, and if a
strong anglophone community could simultaneously be sustained
within Quebec, the separatist impetus would be constrained. Quebec's
francophones would be encouraged to think of themselves as part of
a Canada-wide French-speaking community and would be discour-
aged from associating the French fact with Quebec by the additional
constitutional support given to the survival of an anglophone minority within Quebec.[46]

The eight years from the Constitution Act of 1982 to the demise
of Meech Lake are but a moment in the life-span of constitutions

intended to endure for generations. It may, therefore, be premature to assess the extent to which the political purposes of the Charter have been met. Those eight years, however, were the settling-in period for the Charter and also the era in which the governments of Canada tried and failed to welcome Quebec back into the constitutional family. Finally, the failure of Meech Lake increases the probability of Canada's breakup and thus of the possibility that the Charter may not have a second chance as a nation-building instrument. It is appropriate, therefore, to provide at least a preliminary evaluation of the Charter's success in meeting its political purposes, especially with respect to Quebec. The situation in English Canada is considerably clearer, and we shall first look at it briefly, if tentatively.

THE EVIDENCE FROM PUBLIC HEARINGS convincingly suggests that the Charter has "taken" in English Canada. Particular socio-ethnic categories are powerful defenders of their clause. At a more general level, the Charter is almost an icon, suggesting that it met a need for connection with the constitution that was not met by federalism, parliamentary government, or the monarchy.

The Charter's "taking" in English Canada generates hostility to provincial variations in the availability of rights; hence the rhetorical hostility of federal politicians, including Prime Minister Mulroney, to the notwithstanding clause, presumably reflecting sensitivity to basic public opinion in English Canada and to the latter's specific opposition to Quebec's use of the notwithstanding clause to pass its legislation on the language of signs. The constitutional vision of the Charter was the source of English-Canadian antagonism to Meech Lake's designation of Quebec as a distinct society if that meant differential availability of rights to Canadian citizens in Quebec. In English Canada, therefore, the Charter supports a constitutional norm that is hostile to the provincial diversities natural to federalism if the price is uneven availability of what have come to be seen as attributes of Canadian citizenship. Indeed, from the vantage point of English Canada, the impact of the Charter is precisely its capacity to transform the relation between provincial governments and provincial residents into one between provincial governments and Canadian citizens who happen to reside in a province.

In New Brunswick and Manitoba's public hearings, possibly the most frequent demand was to insulate the Charter against any possible erosion by the accord, especially by the distinct society clause. Over half of the interveners in Manitoba were apprehensive about the Accord's impact on "Charter rights, particularly sex equality rights."[47] The need to define the "Charter's supremacy in the Constitution" was a "major issue" before New Brunswick's Select Committee.[48] For Premier Clyde Wells of Newfoundland, the Charter was "the key component of our Constitution that articulates the fundamental values that define us as Canadians and simply cannot be casually undermined."[49] In a February 1990 poll, 71 per cent of respondents disagreed or strongly disagreed with the statement that "Quebec should have the right to pass laws affecting the distinctive culture and language of Quebec – even if those laws conflict with the Charter of Rights and Freedoms."[50]

The public opinion behind the Charter in English Canada, therefore, limits the capacity of other Canadian governments to give Quebec any unique, constitutionally sanctioned latitude in its application. Since the principle of equality of the provinces hems Quebec in from a different perspective, constitutional principles severely constrain any version of special status for Quebec. Had the Charter been incorporated into the constitutional culture of Quebec's francophone majority, particularly of political élites, as it has been in English Canada, its constraints would be accepted as flowing from collective conscience, rather than as externally imposed.

THE CHARTER'S RECEPTION IN English Canada, however, has not been duplicated among Quebec's francophone majority. The women's movement, for example, was badly split by French-English differences on whether the accord weakened women's Charter rights, especially section 28.[51] Widespread English-Canadian apprehension that the "distinct society" interpretive clause threatened the Charter was not shared by francophone contributors to the Meech Lake debates. They either denied it, implying that the fear concealed a mean-spirited anglophone evaluation of Quebec democracy, or they justified it, on grounds of possible future need for collective measures to protect and nourish a beleaguered linguistic minority. In either case, the passionate English-Canadian–style defences of the Charter were conspicuously absent. The collections of Meech Lake documents, speeches, and so on emanating from Quebec display none of the commitment to the Charter from francophone contributors that is a recurring theme among English-Canadian commentators.

On the contrary, the Charter tends to be seen as a threat to the individuality of Quebec, and the "distinct society" of Meech Lake was positively seen as a defence against the Charter's perceived bias toward homogenization and uniformity.[52] For the Parti québécois, "entrenchment of individual rights in the area of language [aroused deep concern], since such rights could alter the social and cultural priorities reflected in collective rights in that area."[53] Not surprising, therefore, the Charter's purpose of constraining provincial centrifugalism was received less warmly in Quebec, especially in the government, than in English Canada. More generally, the Charter's role as a potent symbol of their Canadian national identity for many English Canadians was reversed for many Québécois, who saw it as a threat to their nationalism. In the cryptic language of one observer: "What is Meech Lake but an effort by Quebec to regain more breathing room under the Charter of rights, which bound it more closely than at any time in our history to a pan-Canadian ideal?"[54]

Quebec's antipathy to the Charter can easily be exaggerated and should not be seen as hostility to the theory and practice of citizens' rights. Nevertheless, the differential reception of the Charter in English Canada and in Quebec is a crucial constitutional phenomenon. It means that, at least in the short run, the national unity purposes of the Charter have not only fallen short but, in a sense, have backfired with respect to relations between Quebec and the rest of Canada. For Quebec's government, Meech Lake was an attempt to escape from some of the Charter's restraints via the "distinct society" clause. For English Canada, that attempted escape was unacceptable precisely because it would have diluted the Charter's impact on Quebec.

The Charter's short history in Quebec has been indelibly marked by the constitutional politics of its origins. It was part of a package that applied to Quebec over the objections of its government. Unavoidably, the Charter became entangled with the nationalists' interpretation of 1980–2 as a betrayal of Quebec. The association of the Charter with betrayal was held with special poignancy by the indépendantistes because they saw it correctly as the central instrument of Trudeau's constitutional vision. Lévesque's hostility to that "bloody Charter,"[55] therefore, was politically understandable. Similarly, the PQ's across-the-board use of the notwithstanding clause – an employment of section 33 not visualized by the Charter's sponsors – gravely weakened the Charter's impact on Quebec's political culture by transmitting the message that Québécois nationalism and the Charter were in opposition. The fact that Quebec's government did not use an equally available override clause in its own provincial Charter of Human Rights and Freedoms, which covered most of the same rights as the federal Charter, clearly indicated that its objection was more to the manner of the Charter's imposition on Quebec than to the rights it contained.[56] It also followed logically that the notwithstanding clause, on the defensive in English Canada, was positively valued in Quebec as an essential weapon against the Charter's antipathy toward provincial diversities.

Two additional factors militated against a positive response to the Charter from the Quebec government and from the francophone majority. First, the Charter became embroiled in the visceral ethnic/

linguistic tensions of Quebec's domestic politics. The anglophone minority used it successfully against restrictive provisions of Bill 101, Quebec's language law.[57] In general, the Charter's impact on Quebec legislation was pronounced and highly visible. The five Quebec statutes struck down on Charter grounds by 1989 were more than for any other province, and they tended to be major statutes dealing with education and language.[58]

For Quebec's government, accordingly, the Charter was an unpredictable and unwelcome intruder. With its capacity to confront majority preferences, or at least the government's view of the long-run linguistic requirements of the francophone majority, with minority rights, it was a potential agent of social disharmony. The Charter was a denial of the nationalist vision of Quebec as a potentially independent French-speaking nation entitled to undertake the measures necessary to ensure its linguistic and cultural survival in the face of the assimilating pressures of an English-speaking continent. As Claude Morin put it, in explaining the PQ opposition to the Charter in 1980–2, Quebec could not tolerate any reduction of its powers by means of the Charter, especially in linguistic matters: "Nothing would make us change our minds."[59] The Charter's negative contribution to problem solving was underlined by the Bourassa government's use of the notwithstanding clause – originally a response to pressure from western governments – to protect its sign legislation against the Charter. This elicited a chorus of disapproval from English Canada that was a major factor in the defeat of Meech Lake.

Second, the two-party domestic politics of Quebec, with an indépendantiste party either in opposition or in government for the last two decades, hinders the acclimatization of Québécois to the Charter as simply part of an accepted constitutional order. No such order exists. Specifically, the Charter's political purposes – to link Québécois more firmly to the constitution and to enhance the Canadian component of the dual identity that federalism fosters among the citizenry – were in direct conflict with the nationalist vision of a healthy political identity based on an undistracted allegiance to the Quebec state and people. PQ hostility to the Canadian Charter as an instrument of a rival philosophy inhibits whatever enthusiasm for the Charter might otherwise appear more natural to the Liberal party,[60] which has alternated in government with the PQ for two decades.

THUS A NUMBER OF REINFORCING factors give the Charter a very different role and profile in francophone Quebec than in English Canada, where it enjoys high status. The Charter, intended to be a force for unity, has not achieved its political purposes.

The search for accommodation between Quebec and the rest of Canada is complicated by differential support for the Charter. In English Canada, the Charter generates a constitutional vision hostile to provincial variations in the rights available to Canadians. This vision, as Meech Lake confirms, inhibits governments in responding positively to Quebec's demands for any distinctive constitutional recognition that appears to encroach on the Charter. The significance of that constraint is compounded by the delegitimation of executive federalism that accompanies it and that denies governments the freedom to act in defiance of public opinion.

The Quebec government is subject to the different, but no less serious constraint of nationalism. Both the Fulton-Favreau formula in the mid-1960s and the Victoria Charter in 1971 were rejected because of nationalist pressures. The rigidity of Quebec's position in the Meech Lake negotiations was a by-product of a two-party system in which the opposition PQ is ever ready to identify the slightest concession as unacceptable weakness, if not betrayal.

The conflict between the nationalist constraint on the Quebec government and the Charter constraint on all the other governments may weaken with time. Logically, two possibilities exist: emerging acceptance in English Canada that the Charter's impact on Quebec should be muted by a more ready resort to the notwithstanding clause than is appropriate elsewhere, coupled with sensitive judicial interpretations that take cognizance of Quebec's distinctiveness; or erosion of the differences in attitudes to the Charter as it gets rooted in Quebec's political culture. This latter cannot be ruled out. Quebec's evolution to a more multicultural and multiracial condition increases the constituency of potential Charter identifiers whose sympathies may spread by intermarriage into the more traditional francophone community. If this happens, the Charter will increasingly enter into the calculations of Quebec's provincial politicians of the future as a force to be reckoned with. This scenario suggests the central importance of Montreal as a meeting point not just of peoples but also of competing constitutional orientations.

The triumph of either of these possibilities presupposes, of course, that a recognizably federal Canada will continue to exist. At the moment, the odds appear to be about fifty-fifty.

CONCLUSION

A humorous postcard I recently received was captioned, "It is difficult to write on a moving planet." It is especially difficult to write constitutions that can speak to posterity for a people that is on the move.

The Canadian society which shapes and is shaped by the constitution does not and will not stand still. Consequently, constitution-making is the site for a contest between inherited patterns of thought and behaviour and new realities that press urgently for recognition. Some of the new realities are transformed old ones – such as Québécois nationalism, provincial assertiveness, and the place of aboriginals in Canadian society. When, however, as in these cases, the old reality puts on new garb, the traditional constitutional response may come to be seen as yesterday's irrelevant answer. Clearly, aboriginal peoples will not return to the invisible off-stage status that was their lot for the first half of the twentieth century. Quebec is unlikely to return to the conservative normality of the pre–Quiet Revolution era, when Duplessis and the Tremblay report defended traditional federalism against centralizing English-Canadian unbelievers. Nor will the provincial governments as a group slip back into the state of impotence and low esteem in which they were held, especially by English-Canadian intellectuals, in the depression. In their different ways, Quebec, other provincial governments, and aboriginal peoples have all evolved to a higher stage of constitutional self-consciousness and efficacy. If these three sources of constitutional discontent were all that we had to resolve, the challenge to our citizenship and states-personship would still be awesomely daunting and intimidating.

Of course, they are not alone. They are joined, as Meech Lake repeatedly underlined, by a new ethnic agenda derived from the ethnic transformation of Canadian society that is making Canadians a new people. We are a multicultural, multiracial, multihistoried, multireligious people, and we will be even more so in the future. The "leading edge" of this transformation, most evident in metropolitan centres, is the recently arrived immigrant population recruited largely from non-traditional source countries. These new arrivals are not guestworkers. They must be treated and conduct themselves as full citizens of a society to whose evolving collective definition they make their own contributions. While they join a historic country, the latter had not fashioned a rigid definition of Canadianism to which all had to adapt. On the contrary, this new immigrant wave inserts itself into a society already undergoing convulsive and incompletely successful attempts to fashion an acceptable constitutional coexistence encompassing French- and English-speaking Canadians, Quebec and the rest of Canada, other nonfounding Canadians, and aboriginal peoples. Almost inadvertently, Canadians have drifted into a situation of ethnic and racial pluralism that makes the state's task of managing society and renewing the consensus of who we are as a people at least as challenging as its task of managing the economy.

That many of our metropolitan classrooms are replicas of the UN general assembly indicates that the traditional French-English–other European–aboriginal ethnic agenda cannot be addressed in isolation from the new immigration-fed ethnicity.

The constitutional import of changing ethnicity and cultural diffusion might have been minimal if our written constitution had been and remained, in Napoleon's phrase, short and obscure. Instead, the Canadian constitution has become increasingly prolix and comprehensive. It has a pervasive ethnic dimension. Aboriginals, visible minorities, European "ethnics," "French-speaking Canadians ... and English-speaking Canadians," in the language of Meech Lake, jostle with each other in the constitution of a country that has two official languages but no official culture. We may come to regret this constitutionalization of ethnicity and come to agree with Napoleon. We cannot, however, escape from the encounter between the constitution and our galloping ethnic and racial pluralism, for we are far from a stable constitutional resting-point.

The second major new force on the constitutional stage, closely linked to our growing ethnic diversity, is the Charter. The Charter is more than a dry technical modification of citizens' rights. It is a consciousness-raising instrument that has profoundly changed Canadian constitutional culture. The Charter and the constitutional identities that it created, along with the participatory impulses that it stimulated, were largely responsible – with a significant assist from the aboriginal peoples – for repudiation of the executive federalism–style Meech Lake process. The Charter has greatly enlarged the cast of constitutional actors. This Charter-led attack on government dominance of the formal amending process pulls Canadians in the direction of a major constitutional debate on the location of sovereignty. That the Charter – still in its infancy and a constitutional instrument that for most of our history would have been rejected as un-British and therefore un-Canadian – has already had such far-reaching consequences suggests that it has an institutional charisma not possessed by federalism and parliamentary government.

The constitutional vision inspired by the Charter, however, also generated hostility in the rest of Canada to Meech Lake's definition of Quebec as a distinct society and to the role of the Quebec government and legislature "to preserve and promote the distinct identity of Quebec" and thus to escape in part from the Charter's grasp. At least in the short run, therefore, the Charter has failed in its purpose as an instrument of Canadian unity. It has not weakened Québécois nationalism or developed into a common bond of positive constitutional identification that unites Canadians across the historic French-

English divide. Its reception in English Canada, however, means that a more participatory process than Meech Lake is essential if a constitutional settlement is to have legitimacy. It follows logically that there are limits to the encroachments on the Charter that such a settlement can contain.

Whatever its short- or long-range failing in bridging the gaps between Quebec and the rest of Canada, French and English, however, the Charter is an instructive and positive example of constitutional theorizing and implementation. It indicates that remarkable changes in the constitutional life of a people can be introduced and digested in a very short period. We are not restricted to small-scale incrementalism, and we can go outside the confines of our traditions, narrowly defined, in our search for answers to the perplexing questions on our agenda. We might even find the necessary courage to be daringly creative if we remembered that the components of our inheritance were, perhaps long ago, new creations.

Constitution-makers should begin their meetings with the wise words of Václav Havel: "Society is a very mysterious animal with many faces and hidden potentialities, and ... it's extremely short-sighted to believe that the face society happens to be presenting to you at a given moment is its only true face. None of us knows all the potentialities that slumber in the spirit of the population, or all the ways in which that population can surprise us when there is the right interplay of events, both visible and invisible ... One must be very careful about coming to any conclusions about the way we are, or what can be expected of us."[61]

Notes

ACKNOWLEDGMENTS

1 Erving Goffman, *Forms of Talk* (Philadelphia 1981), chap. 4, "The Lecture."

INTRODUCTION

1 My indebtedness to Robert Jackson, Samuel LaSelva, and Cynthia and Douglas Williams for many of the ideas in this book is gratefully acknowledged. My references in these notes do not do justice to their contribution to my understanding.
2 Technically, the "multicultural heritage" refers to all Canadians. Politically, however, it is seen as applying primarily to Third Force Canadians and to visible minorities, excluding the aboriginal, French, and English peoples.
3 While the terminology of section 28 is neutral, referring to both male and female persons, it is conventionally thought of as the women's clause.
4 Cited in R.J. Vincent, *Human Rights and International Relations* (Cambridge, UK, 1986), 17.
5 For the counterargument that the practice of rights is hostile to democratic participation, see Charles Taylor, "Alternative Futures: Legitimacy, Identity and Alienation in Late Twentieth Century Canada," in Alan Cairns and Cynthia Williams, eds., *Constitutionalism, Citizenship and Society in Canada*, Vol. 33 of the research studies of the Royal Commission on the Economic Union and Development Prospects for Canada (Toronto 1985).
6 See Alan C. Cairns, "Citizens (Outsiders) and Governments (Insiders) in Constitution-Making: The Case of Meech Lake," *Canadian Public Policy* 14 supplement (Sept. 1988): s125–7.

7 Alan C. Cairns, "The Canadian Constitutional Experiment," *Dalhousie Law Journal* 9 (Nov. 1984): 98.

8 The concessions are in section 6 (mobility rights) and in section 1 (reasonable limits clause) and section 33 (notwithstanding clause), although the latter (1 and 33) apply to both orders of government. Section 59 of the Constitution Act, 1982, delays the application to Quebec of section 23 (1)(a), dealing with one category of minority-language educational rights, until the legislative assembly or government of Quebec so authorizes.

9 Samuel LaSelva, "Does the Canadian Charter of Rights and Freedoms Rest on a Mistake?" *Windsor Yearbook of Access to Justice* 8 (1988): 223.

10 L.S. Lustgarten, "Liberty in a Culturally Plural Society," in A. Phillips Griffiths, ed., *Of Liberty* (Cambridge, UK, 1983), 98.

11 Alan C. Cairns, "The Governments and Societies of Canadian Federalism," *Canadian Journal of Political Science* 10 (Dec. 1977): 695–725, and "The Other Crisis of Canadian Federalism," *Canadian Public Administration* 22 (summer 1979): 175–95.

CHAPTER ONE

1 Peter Gourevitch, "The Second Image Reversed: The International Sources of Domestic Politics," *International Organization* 32 (autumn 1978): 911.

2 Theda Skocpol, "Bringing the State back in: Strategies of Analysis in Current Research," in Peter B. Evans, Dietrich Rueschemeyer, and Theda Skocpol, *Bringing the State back in* (Cambridge, Mass., 1985), 8.

3 Robert J. Jackson et al., *Politics in Canada: Culture, Institutions, Behaviour and Public Policy* (Scarborough, Ont., 1986), 44.

4 Oran R. Young, "Interdependencies in World Politics," in Ray Maghroori and Bennett Ramberg, eds., *Globalism versus Realism: International Relations' Third Debate* (Boulder, Col., 1982), 65–6.

5 Ray Maghroori, "Introduction: Major Debates in International Relations," in Maghroori and Ramberg, eds., *Globalism versus Realism*, 14.

6 Alexander Brady, "Canada and the Model of Westminster," in William B. Hamilton, ed., *The Transfer of Institutions* (Durham, NC, 1964), 67–8.

7 John W. Holmes, *The Shaping of Peace: Canada and the Search for World Order 1943–1957*, Vol. 1 (Toronto 1979), 303.

8 *Report: Royal Commission on the Economic Union and Development Prospects for Canada*, Vol. 1 (Ottawa 1985), 62.

9 Kent Roach, "The Intellectual and Political Origins of the Canadian Bill of Rights, 1945–60," unpublished ms., mimeo, 1984, 17, 65.

10 Data from Elliot L. Tepper, "Demographic Change and Pluralism," in

O.P. Dwivedi et al, eds., *Canada 2000: Race Relations and Public Policy* (Guelph 1989), and Gilles Paquet, "Multiculturalism as National Policy," *Journal of Cultural Economics* 13 (June 1989): 21–2.

11 David R. Cameron, "Lord Durham Then and Now," *Journal of Canadian Studies* 25 (spring 1990): 15. This stimulating paper, which came to my attention in draft form while I was revising this chapter, has helped to clarify my thoughts in a number of areas.

12 T. John Samuel, "Immigration, Visible Minorities and the Labour Force in Canada: Vision 2000," in Dwivedi et al, eds., *Canada 2000*, 182.

13 Raymond Breton, "From Ethnic to Civic Nationalism: The Experience of English Canada and Quebec," mimeo, Sept. 1987, 17.

14 Alan C. Cairns, "The Judicial Committee and Its Critics," *Canadian Journal of Political Science* 4 (Sept. 1971): 301–45.

15 Roach, "Origins," 90–1.

16 R.M. Dawson, *Democratic Government in Canada*, revised by W.F. Dawson (Toronto 1963), 14.

17 This intellectual tendency was most evident in left-wing interpretations of the Canadian party system from the 1930s to the 1960s, and entered into John Porter's plea for "creative politics" in *The Vertical Mosaic* (Toronto 1965).

18 See Edward McWhinney, *Judicial Review in the English-Speaking World* (Toronto 1956), for a pioneering early work by this prolific author.

19 J. Noel Lyon and Ronald G. Atkey, eds., *Canadian Constitutional Law in a Modern Perspective* (Toronto 1970).

20 Donald Smiley, "The Structural Problem of Canadian Federalism," *Canadian Public Administration* 14 (fall 1971): 326–43.

21 Roger Gibbins, *Regionalism: Territorial Politics in Canada and the United States* (Toronto 1982). For a general survey of the intrastate analysis see Donald V. Smiley and Ronald L. Watts, *Intrastate Federalism in Canada*, Vol. 39 of the research studies of the Royal Commission on the Economic Union and Development Prospects for Canada (Toronto 1985).

22 Smiley, "Structural Problem," 339–40 ("A Brief Digression: The American Experience").

23 Gerrit W. Gong, *The Standard of 'Civilization' in International Society* (Oxford 1984), 246.

24 Daniel J. Elazar, ed., *Federalism and Political Integration* (Ramat Gan, Israel, 1979), 4.

25 Robert H. Jackson, "Quasi-States: Sovereignty, International Relations and the Third World," unpub. ms., chap. 6, p. 7. See also R.J. Vincent, "Racial Equality," in Hedley Bull and Adam Watson, eds., *The Expansion of International Society* (Oxford 1984).

26 *Re Drummond Wren* (1945) OR 778 (HC).

27 R. Kenneth Carty and W. Peter Ward, "The Making of a Canadian Political Citizenship," in R. Kenneth Carty and W. Peter Ward, eds., *National Politics and Community in Canada* (Vancouver 1986), 74.

28 Cited in Roach, "Origins," 15.

29 The non-white members also used the Commonwealth to apply pressure on the United Kingdom to accelerate decolonization. Jackson, "Quasi-States," chap. 4, 24.

30 John W. Holmes, *The Shaping of Peace: Canada and the Search for World Order 1943–1957*, Vol. 2 (Toronto 1982), 169, 171–2.

31 R.J. Vincent, *Human Rights and International Relations* (Cambridge, UK, 1986), 130.

32 Ivo D. Duchacek, "Federalist Responses to Ethnic Demands: An Overview," in Elazar, ed., *Federalism*, 64.

33 J.D.B. Miller, "The Sovereign State and Its Future," *International Journal* 39 (spring 1984): 286.

34 René Lévesque, "We Are Quebeckers," An Address given by Mr. René Lévesque, Prime Minister of Quebec, Before the Members of the Assemblée Nationale, Paris, 2 Nov. 1977, mimeo, 14.

35 Cameron, "Lord Durham Then and Now," 17.

36 Maxwell Cohen, "Human Rights: Programme or Catchall? A Canadian Rationale," *Canadian Bar Review* 46 (Dec. 1968): 554.

37 Ibid., 557.

38 See Allan Gotlieb, ed., *Human Rights, Federalism and Minorities* (Toronto 1970), for helpful analyses of the UN's impact on the theory and practice of rights in Canada. According to one contributor, Ivan Head ("Regional Developments Respecting Human Rights: The Implications for Canada," 243), the world in which Canadians could believe in "parliamentary supremacy and judicial non-intervention ... changed forever ... in 1945 when Canada, with forty-nine others (now more than 120), determined '... to reaffirm faith in fundamental human rights, in the dignity and worth of the human person, in the equal rights of men and women ... and for these ends ... to employ international machinery for the promotion of the economic and social advancement of all peoples.'"

39 Vincent, *Human Rights*, 93.

40 Jackson, "Quasi-States," chap 2, p. 14.

41 Vincent, *Human Rights*, 97–9.

42 Holmes, *The Shaping of Peace*, Vol. 1, 290–5.

43 *Journals of the Senate of Canada*, No. 62, 27 June 1950, 434.

44 Brooke Jeffrey, "The Charter of Rights and Freedoms and Its Effect on Canadians," Library of Parliament Background Paper, Ottawa 1982, 8.

45 John Claydon, "International Human Rights Law and the Interpretation of the Canadian Charter of Rights and Freedoms," *Supreme Court Law Review* 4 (1982): 287.

46 Ibid., 288 n. 4.

47 See Allan Gotlieb, "The Changing Canadian Attitude to the United Nations Role in Protecting and Developing Human Rights," 16–53, in Gotlieb, ed., *Human Rights*, for an analysis of the Canadian response to this "federalism" question.

48 John Boli-Bennett, "Human Rights or State Expansion? Cross-National Definitions of Constitutional Rights, 1870–1970," in Ved P. Nanda et al, eds., *Global Human Rights: Public Policies, Comparative Measures, and NGO Strategies* (Boulder, Col., 1981).

49 Hugh Collins, as cited in Peter H. Russell, "The Politics of Frustration: The Pursuit of Formal Constitutional Change in Australia and Canada," *Australian-Canadian Studies* 6, no.1 (1988): 22.

50 Vincent, *Human Rights*, 103.

51 L. Neville Brown, "A Bill of Rights for the United Kingdom?" *The Parliamentarian* 58 (1977): 85. The Brown article is a useful summary of developing pressure in Britain up to the mid-1970s for a Bill of Rights, including the advocacy of Lords Scarman and Hailsham.

52 Gong, *The Standard of 'Civilization,'* 91. Ian Brownlie asserts that "there is indeed a considerable support for the view that there is in international law today a legal principle of non-discrimination which at the least applies in matters of race"; *Principles of Public International Law,* 3rd ed. (Oxford 1979), 596.

53 Vincent, *Human Rights*, 152.

54 Stephen D. Krasner, "Approaches to the State: Alternative Conceptions and Historical Dynamics," *Comparative Politics* 16 (Jan. 1984): 241.

55 Gourevitch, "The Second Image Reversed," 900.

CHAPTER TWO

1 Charles Tilly, "Studying the Ends of Wars," *States and Social Structures Newsletter* (fall 1986): 1.

2 Some of the material in this section repeats the analysis in an unpublished paper presented to the Round Table on Politics and Ethnicity, International Political Science Association, Oxford, 26–28 March 1979: Alan C. Cairns, "French-English Conflict in Canada: The Ambiguous Role of Institutions."

3 Gerald M. Craig, ed., *Lord Durham's Report: An Abridgement of Report on the Affairs of British North America* (Toronto 1963), 150, 146.

4 David R. Cameron, "Lord Durham Then and Now," *Journal of Canadian Studies* 25 (spring 1990): 9.

5 John D. Whyte, "Reinventing Canada: The Meaning of Constitutional Change," mimeo, Public Law Workshops, Osgoode Hall Law School, York University, n.d., 14.

6 "We Are Quebeckers," An Address Given by Mr. René Lévesque, Prime Minister of Quebec, before the Members of the Assemblée Nationale, Paris, 2 Nov. 1977, mimeo, 13.

7 "The Province of Quebec is isolated within nine provinces which are solidly and eternally anglophone. Even in New Brunswick, which has the largest francophone minority, the proportion is only 35 per cent of the population. Quebec is the only province which faces a federal government which it can never control because the majority – by which I mean the anglophone majority – determines the decisions made by the federal government ... [and the taxes Quebec pays to Ottawa go] to fill the purse of a government which primarily reflects the needs of the nine anglophone provinces. Certainly this majority is not necessarily opposed to us but it almost always, logically, serves itself first ... in order to ensure its development." René Lévesque, *My Quebec* (Toronto 1979), 117–18.

8 Richard Handler, *Nationalism and the Politics of Culture in Quebec* (Madison 1988), 31, citing René Lévesque.

9 Ibid., 5, citing two Quebec government publications.

10 Ibid., 48–9.

11 Lévesque, "We Are Quebeckers," 12.

12 Claude Morin, *Quebec versus Ottawa: The Struggle for Self-Government 1960–72* (Toronto 1976), 130.

13 Kenneth McRoberts, *Quebec: Social Change and Political Crisis*, 3rd ed. (Toronto 1988), 257–8.

14 Lévesque, *My Québec*, 74.

15 Quoted in Handler, *Nationalism,* 179.

16 McRoberts, *Quebec,* 327.

17 Cited in "Sovereignty-Association: A Backgrounder," Government of Quebec, mimeo, n.d., 6.

18 Government of Quebec, *Québec-Canada: A New Deal* (Quebec City 1979), 42.

19 The Task Force on Canadian Unity, *A Future Together: Observations and Recommendations* (Ottawa 1979), 48.

20 J.R. Mallory, "The Continuing Evolution of Canadian Constitutionalism," in Alan Cairns and Cynthia Williams, eds., *Constitutionalism, Citizenship and Society in Canada,* Vol. 33 of the research studies of the Royal Commission on the Economic Union and Development Prospects for Canada (Toronto 1985), p. 87.

21 K.C. Wheare, *Federal Government,* 3rd ed. (London 1953), 20.

22 Donald V. Smiley, "The Structural Problem of Canadian Federalism," *Canadian Public Administration* 14 (autumn 1971): 334.

23 Canada West Foundation, *Follow-Up on Alternatives Canada Conference Banff, March 27–29, 1978* (Calgary 1978), 6.

24 Donald V. Smiley, "Territorialism and Canadian Political Institutions," *Canadian Public Policy* 3 (autumn 1977): 456.

25 Although the concept of instructed provincial-government delegates was derived from the German Bundesrat, it had indigenous roots in Canada's western agrarian protest movements of the early twentieth century. The theory and practice of the recall, under which MPs signed undated resignations that could be dated should their fidelity to their constituents slacken, reflected a similar desire to keep representatives on a leash. Both the recall and provincialist intrastate proposals reflected the antipathy of minorities to majoritarianism and the fear that representatives, left to themselves or subject to party discipline, could not be trusted to speak for the constituents or governments that had sent them to Ottawa.

26 Richard Vernon, "The Federal Citizen," in R.D. Olling and M.W. Westmacott, eds., *Perspectives on Canadian Federalism* (Scarborough, Ont., 1988) 3–15.

27 Jennifer Smith, "Intrastate Federalism and Confederation," in Stephen Brooks, ed., *Political Thought in Canada: Contemporary Perspectives* (Toronto 1984), 271–2.

28 Marc Lalonde, *Constitutional Reform: House of the Federation* (Ottawa 1978).

29 See Alan C. Cairns, "Constitution-Making, Government Self-Interest, and the Problem of Legitimacy," in Allan Kornberg and Harold D. Clarke, eds., *Political Support in Canada: The Crisis Years* (Durham, NC, 1983), 423–8, for the complexities of the federal position and its evolution prior to the Supreme Court's decision on the constitutionality of unilateralism. See also Stephen A. Scott, "The Canadian Constitutional Amendment Process: Mechanisms and Prospects," in Clare F. Beckton and A. Wayne MacKay, eds., *Recurring Issues in Canadian Federalism*, Vol. 57 of the research studies of the Royal Commission on the Economic Union and Development Prospects for Canada (Toronto 1986) 77–111.

30 Peter H. Russell, "The Politics of Frustration: The Pursuit of Formal Constitutional Change in Australia and Canada," *Australian-Canadian Studies* 6, no. 1 (1988): 16.

31 From the Constitutional Conference of February 1968 "until the final enactment of the Constitution Act, 1982, giving constitutional expression to fundamental rights including language rights was the Trudeau government's first constitutional priority. And throughout, the fundamental basic rationale for this constitutional strategy was the perceived value of such a measure as a popular and unifying counter to decentralizing provincial demands in the Canadian constitutional debate." Peter H. Russell, "The Political Purposes of the Canadian Charter of Rights and Freedoms," *Canadian Bar Review* 61 (March 1983): 33.

32 Handler, *Nationalism*, 183, cites Quebec studies that confirm how Bill
101 has attracted immigrant children to the French-language school
system in Montreal but were apprehensive that the Canada clause in
the 1982 Charter might "reverse the trend."

33 Cited in Kent Roach, "The Intellectual and Political Origins of the
Canadian Bill of Rights, 1945–60," unpub. ms., 1984, 79.

34 Technically, the federal government's amending proposal was not to be
implemented as part of the patriation package but was to be accepted
or rejected in a complex series of post-patriation procedures guaranteed to produce an amending formula. However, the latter were biased
in favour of the federal formula. I simply describe the federal amending proposals as the federal formula, without constantly qualifying that
phrase by a reminder of the complex process through which it might
or might not be adopted. For details see Cairns, "Constitution-Making,"
423–8.

35 There were some modifications in the federal formula as the government responded to criticisms and refined certain details. See ibid. for
particulars.

36 This assumes that any absence of provincial legislative approval would
reflect a provincial government's unwillingness to obtain it – not always
a safe assumption, given the frequency of minority governments.

37 Cairns, "Constitution-Making," 439.

38 Russell, "Politics of Frustration," 8–9.

39 McRoberts, *Quebec*, 353–4.

40 In addition to the points noted below, see the insightful discussion of
Patrick Macklem, "Constitutional Ideologies," *Ottawa Law Review* 20, no.
1 (1988): 117–56, which could also be applied to the reform proposals
discussed above.

41 Keith G. Banting and Richard Simeon, eds., *The Politics of Constitutional
Change in Industrial Nations: Redesigning the State* (London 1985), 26.

42 *Report of the Royal Commission of Inquiry on Constitutional Problems* (Quebec 1956).

43 Quebec, *Québec-Canada*.

44 Gilles Paquet, "Pour une notion renouvelée de citoyenneté," prononcé
au colloque "Nationalisme et diversité culturelle au Québec," Université
Laval, miméo, le 7 juin 1989, 6.

45 Raymond Breton, "From Ethnic to Civic Nationalism: The Experience
of English Canada and Quebec," mimeo, Sept. 1987.

46 Cited in John W. Holmes, *The Shaping of Peace: Canada and the Search
for World Order 1943–1957*, Vol. 1 (Toronto 1979), 77–8.

47 Michael Walzer, "The Distribution of Membership," in Peter G. Brown
and Henry Shue, eds., *Boundaries: National Autonomy and Its Limits*
(Totowa, NJ, 1981), 2.

48 Elsa M. Chaney, "Migrant Workers and National Boundaries," in Brown and Shue, eds., *Boundaries*, 38.

49 See Samuel V. LaSelva, "Does the Canadian Charter of Rights and Freedoms Rest on a Mistake?" *Windsor Yearbook of Access to Justice* 8 (1988), for a stimulating discussion.

50 Gilles Paquet, "Multiculturalism as National Policy," *Journal of Cultural Economics* 13 (June 1989): 25.

CHAPTER THREE

1 Keith Banting and Richard Simeon, eds., *And No One Cheered: Federalism, Democracy and the Constitution Act* (Toronto 1983).

2 Alan C. Cairns, "The Limited Constitutional Vision of Meech Lake," in Katherine E. Swinton and Carol J. Rogerson, eds., *Competing Constitutional Visions: The Meech Lake Accord* (Toronto 1988), 261.

3 Peter H. Russell, "The Politics of Frustration: The Pursuit of Formal Constitutional Change in Australia and Canada," *Australian-Canadian Studies*, 6, no. 1 (1988): 14.

4 For a preliminary exploration, see Alan C. Cairns, "Political Science, Ethnicity, and the Canadian Constitution," in David P. Shugarman and Reg Whitaker, eds., *Federalism and Political Community: Essays in Honour of Donald Smiley* (Peterborough, Ont., 1989), 113–40.

5 Robert C. Vipond, "Whatever Became of the Compact Theory? Meech Lake and the New Politics of Constitutional Amendment in Canada," *Queen's Quarterly* 96 (winter 1989): 793–811.

6 Janet Hiebert, "The Evolution of 'Reasonable Limits' in the Charter," mimeo, prepared for the Annual Meeting, Canadian Political Science Association, University of Windsor, June 1988.

7 W.R. Lederman, "Democratic Parliaments, Independent Courts and the Canadian Charter of Rights and Freedoms," in John C. Courtney, ed., *The Canadian House of Commons: Essays in Honour of Norman Ward* (Calgary 1985), 89–111.

8 He continues: "For legislators, rather than judges, bear the exclusive responsibility for the enactment of laws, and most laws are either never tested in courts or receive limited judicial scrutiny only after being in force for a number of years." Samuel V. LaSelva, "Only in Canada: Federalism, *Non Obstante*, and the Charter," in R.D. Olling and M.W. Westmacott, eds., *Perspectives on Canadian Federalism* (Scarborough 1988), 81.

9 J.R. Mallory, for example, states that "the existence of the Charter has already affected police and law-enforcement procedures: much greater care is now exercised to ensure that the accused are apprised of their rights, that searches are legal, and that evidence is not tainted by dubi-

ous investigative and interrogating procedures. Second, a more scrupulous judicial scrutiny of the procedural aspects of law will impel those drafting legislation and regulations to adhere to the principles of the Charter." "The Continuing Evolution of Canadian Constitutionalism," in Alan C. Cairns and Cynthia Williams, eds., *Constitutionalism, Citizenship and Society in Canada*, Vol. 33 of the research studies of the Royal Commission on the Economic Union and Development Prospects for Canada (Toronto 1985), 91.

10 This point is made explicitly in the presentation of the Canadian Association of Law Teachers on the Meech Lake Accord. *Minutes of Proceedings and Evidence of the Special Joint Committee of the Senate and of the House of Commons on the 1987 Constitutional Accord*, No. 15, 31 Aug. 1987.

11 Paul M. Sniderman, Joseph F. Fletcher, Peter H. Russell, and Philip E. Tetlock are involved in a major research project on the Charter's impact on the values and identities of Canadians. An initial publication on one aspect of their findings is "Political Culture and the Problem of Double Standards: Mass and Elite Attitudes toward Language Rights in the Canadian Charter of Rights and Freedoms," *Canadian Journal of Political Science* 22 (June 1989): 259–84.

12 That openness, however, is selective. In spite of the efforts of the Canadian Association of Lesbians and Gay Men, neither the Joint Committee nor the federal government was prepared to add homosexuality or sexual orientation as one of the categories in section 15 specifically identified as entitled to equality rights.

13 Deborah Coyne, "Amending the Constitution of Canada: Who Says You Can't Eat Meech Lake?," notes for remarks to the 12th Seminar, Canadian Regional Commonwealth Parliamentary Association, 1987, mimeo, 8.

14 John Whyte, "Reinventing Canada: The Meaning of Constitutional Change," mimeo, Public Law Workshop, Osgoode Hall Law School, York University, n.d., 18, 28.

15 Allan C. Hutchinson and Andrew Petter, "Private Rights/Public Wrongs: The Liberal Lie of the Charter," *University of Toronto Law Journal* 38 (summer 1988): 283. I am grateful to Stephanie Hudson for drawing this reference to my attention.

16 Ibid.

17 Andrew Petter, "Immaculate Deception: The Charter's Hidden Agenda," *Advocate* 45 (Nov. 1987): 857.

18 Charles Taylor, "Alternative Futures: Legitimacy, Identity and Alienation in Late Twentieth Century Canada," in Cairns and Williams, eds., *Constitutionalism*, 183–229.

19 Roderick A. Macdonald, "Procedural Due Process in Canadian Constitutional Law: Natural Justice and Fundamental Justice," *University of Florida Law Review* 39 (spring 1987): 265.

20 Patrick Monahan, *Politics and the Constitution: The Charter, Federalism and the Supreme Court of Canada* (Toronto 1987), 13.

21 David J. Elkins, "Facing Our Destiny: Rights and Canadian Distinctiveness," *Canadian Journal of Political Science* 22 (Dec. 1989): 699–716.

22 Thomas R. Berger, "Towards the Regime of Tolerance," in Stephen Brooks, ed., *Political Thought in Canada: Contemporary Perspectives* (Toronto 1984), 83–96.

23 Bibliography in Gérald-A. Beaudoin and Ed Ratushny, eds., *The Canadian Charter of Rights and Freedoms*, 2nd ed. (Toronto 1989), 843–921.

24 Cited in Roger Gibbins, Rainer Knopff, and F.L. Morton, "Canadian Federalism, the Charter of Rights, and the 1984 Election," *Publius: The Journal of Federalism* 15 (summer 1985): 165.

25 See Mr Justice Brian Dickson, "The Public Responsibilities of Lawyers," *Manitoba Law Journal* 13 (1983): 179–80, for the role of legal scholarship in the judicial process.

26 According to Peter Russell, the Supreme Court's explicit message to the legal community and to lower courts in early cases from mid-1984 to early 1986 was that "the Charter was not to be treated as the Canadian Bill of Rights had been." "Canada's Charter of Rights and Freedoms: A Political Report," *Public Law* (autumn 1988): 389.

27 Peter H. Russell, "The First Three Years in Charterland," *Canadian Public Administration* 28 (autumn 1985): 372–3.

28 Marc Gold, "The Rhetoric of Rights: The Supreme Court and the Charter," *Osgoode Hall Law Journal* 25 (summer 1987): 379–80.

29 A Gallup poll in spring 1981 showed that 62 per cent of Canadians supported the idea of including a Charter in the patriation plan and only 15 per cent were opposed. There was little regional variation in support. Reg Whitaker, "Democracy and the Canadian Constitution," in Banting and Simeon, eds., *And No One Cheered*, 254.

30 F.L. Morton, "The Political Impact of the Canadian Charter of Rights and Freedoms," *Canadian Journal of Political Science* 20 (March 1987): 34.

31 F.L. Morton and M.J. Withey, "Charting the Charter, 1982–1985: A Statistical Analysis," Occasional Papers Series, Research Unit for Socio-Legal Studies, University of Calgary, Research Study 2.1 (Sept. 1986), 2.

32 Russell, "The First Three Years," 386–94.

33 Morton and Withey, "Charting the Charter," 6.

34 Coyne, "Amending the Constitution," 6.

35 Clifford Geertz, *Negara: The Theatre State in Nineteenth-Century Bali* (Princeton, NJ, 1980).
36 Raymond Breton, "The Production and Allocation of Symbolic Resources: An Analysis of the Linguistic and Ethnocultural Fields in Canada," *Canadian Review of Sociology and Anthropology* 21 (May 1984): 125.
37 Gold, "The Rhetoric of Rights," 399.
38 Ibid., 377. This is the rights version of Paquet's thesis that multiculturalism is "redrawing mental maps and redefining levels of aspirations ... [which] modifies the frame of mind" of ethnic communities. Gilles Paquet, "Multiculturalism as National Policy," *Journal of Cultural Economics* 13 (June 1989): 25.
39 Gibbins, Knopff and Morton, "Canadian Federalism," 162.
40 Ibid., 163.
41 Russell, "The First Three Years," 380.
42 Ronald L. Watts, "Divergence and Convergence: Canadian and U.S. Federalism," in Harry M. Scheiber, ed., *Perspectives on Federalism: Papers from the First Berkeley Seminar on Federalism* (Berkeley: Institute of Intergovernmental Studies, 1987), 194–5.
43 Section "23. (1) Citizens of Canada (a) whose first language learned and still understood is that of the English or French linguistic minority population of the province in which they reside ... have the right to have their children receive primary and secondary school instruction in that language in that province."
44 F.L. Morton et al, "Judicial Nullification of Statutes under the Charter of Rights and Freedoms, 1982–1988," mimeo, prepared for a joint session of the Annual Meetings of the Canadian Political Science Association and the Canadian Law and Society Association, Quebec City, 3 June 1989. Although the number of nullified provincial statutes, at thirty-three, is only marginally greater than the thirty-two federal statutes affected, the former were more likely to have been enacted recently and to involve "substantive" rather than procedural grounds.
45 Russell, "Canada's Charter," 394–5.
46 Peter H. Russell, "The Political Purposes of the Canadian Charter of Rights and Freedoms," *Canadian Bar Review* 61 (March 1983), 51–2.
47 J. Peter Meekison, "The Amending Formula," in Olling and Westmacott, eds., *Perspectives*, 66. Stephen A. Scott identifies five categories only, by classifying the removal of the Senate's veto as a subcategory; "The Canadian Constitutional Amendment Process: Mechanisms and Prospects," in Clare F. Beckton and A. Wayne MacKay, eds., *Recurring Issues in Canadian Federalism*, Vol. 57 of the research studies of the Royal Commission on the Economic Union and Development Prospects for Canada (Toronto 1986), 82–5.

48 However, the Senate's veto remains with respect to amendments under section 44. Scott's phrasing is helpful: "Section 47 denies the Senate full coordinate authority in all the bilateral and multilateral procedures." "The Amendment Process," 84.

49 Section 41 requires unanimity for the following:
"(a) the office of the Queen, the Governor General and the Lieutenant Governor of a province;
(b) the right of a province to a number of members in the House of Commons not less than the number of Senators by which the province is entitled to be represented at the time this Part comes into force;
(c) subject to section 43, the use of the English or the French language;
(d) the composition of the Supreme Court of Canada; and
(e) an amendment to this Part" (dealing with the amending procedure).

50 Meekison, "The Amending Formula," 67.

51 The provincial proposal that provinces opting out of an amendment transferring legislative responsibility to the federal government would receive "reasonable compensation" from Ottawa was restricted to amendments relating to "education or other cultural matters." The Gang of Eight's proposal for delegation of legislative authority was also dropped.

52 B.L. Strayer, "Amendment of the Canadian Constitution: Why the Fulton-Favreau Formula?" *Canadian Legal Studies* 3 (May 1966): 119.

53 Meekison, "The Amending Formula," 67.

54 Alan C. Cairns, "The Canadian Constitutional Experiment," *Dalhousie Law Journal* 9 (Nov. 1984): 100.

55 Scott, "The Amendment Process," 88.

56 "Amending Formula for the Constitution of Canada: Text and Explanatory Notes," Ottawa, 16 April 1981 (amending formula proposed by the governments of the Gang of Eight dissenting provinces).

57 Coyne, "Amending the Constitution," 9.

58 Vipond, "Whatever Became of the Compact Theory?" 797–804.

59 Richard Simeon, "Meech Lake and Shifting Conceptions of Canadian Federalism," *Canadian Public Policy*, 14 supplement (Sept. 1988): s22.

60 Mallory, "The Continuing Evolution," 93–4.

CHAPTER FOUR

1 The main positions in the "betrayal" controversy are argued vigorously by Marcel Adam, Pierre Trudeau, and Claude Morin in Donald Johnston, ed., *Lac Meech: Trudeau parle ... textes réunis et présentés par Donald Johnston* (Montreal 1989), 121–50.

2 Lowell Murray, "The Process of Constitutional Change in Canada: The Lessons of Meech Lake," *Choices,* Institute for Research on Public Policy, Feb. 1988: n.p.

3 Graham Fraser, "PM Says 1982 Flaws Removed 'Flexibility' in Meech Lake Talks," *Globe and Mail*, 13 June 1988; Lowell Murray, letter to editor, *Globe and Mail*, 17 May 1989.

4 I have made a preliminary attempt at anthropological understanding in "Constitutional Minoritarianism in Canada," J.A. Corry Lecture, Queen's University, 6 March 1990.

5 Keith G. Banting, "Federalism and the Supreme Court of Canada: The Contradictions of Legitimation," mimeo, prepared for Ontario Law Reform Commission, Conference on the Nomination of Persons for Judicial Appointment, 14–15 Sept. 1989, Kingston, Ont., 19 and n. 33, citing Dale C. Thomson, *Louis St. Laurent: Canadian* (Toronto 1967), 277.

6 Keith Banting and Richard Simeon, eds., *And No One Cheered: Federalism, Democracy and the Constitution Act* (Toronto 1983).

7 For a discussion, see J. Peter Meekison, "The Amending Formula," in R.D. Olling and M.W. Westmacott, eds., *Perspectives on Canadian Federalism* (Scarborough, Ont., 1988), 61–76.

8 Graham Fraser, "Premiers Who Oppose Accord 'Desire a Solution,' Minister Says," *Globe and Mail*, 8 Jan. 1990.

9 "Meech Discord Report Rouses PM," *Vancouver Sun*, 8 March 1988; Graham Fraser, "PM Says 1982 Flaws Removed 'Flexibility' in Meech Lake Talks," *Globe and Mail*, 13 June 1988.

10 See Robert M. Campbell, "Eleven Men and a Constitution: The Meech Lake Accord," in Robert M. Campbell and Leslie A. Pal, eds., *The Real Worlds of Canadian Politics: Cases in Process and Policy* (Peterborough 1989), 288–89, for a succinct analysis of the efforts to keep the process tightly controlled.

11 Murray, "Process."

12 In Manitoba, the hearings were undertaken not by a legislative committee but by an all-party task force.

13 The Senate held its major hearings in Committee of the Whole, thus ensuring their wide circulation in the published Senate debates. The cast of witnesses was enlarged by setting up an additional submissions group. (See Senate [1988], *Proceedings of the Senate Submissions Group on the Meech Lake Constitutional Accord*). A separate task force was established as a special outlet for aggrieved Northerners. (See Senate Task Force 1987–88, *Proceedings of the Senate Task Force on the Meech Lake Constitutional Accord and on the Yukon and the Northwest Territories*.)

14 "The Opposition to Meech: The Recalcitrants or the Amending Formula?" *Language and Society* 31 (summer 1990): 9.

15 Geoffrey York, "Western NDP Leaders Unite against Meech," *Globe and Mail*, 3 March 1989. In Alberta, the NDP had its own hearings on the accord, in a protest against the government's unwillingness to do so. It

received one hundred and fifty submissions, "all but one of which expressed deep concern about the accord." Campbell, "Eleven Men and a Constitution," p. 281. Michael Harcourt, British Columbia's NDP leader, subsequently stated that despite his concerns he would not rescind the legislature's approval of the accord if he became premier. Jeff Buttle and Keith Baldrey, "Vander Zalm Not Sure Meech Can Be Ratified," *Vancouver Sun*, 23 March 1990.

16 Geoffrey York, "Western Liberals Unite for Campaign," *Globe and Mail*, 19 July 1989.

17 Susan Delacourt, "Meech Lake Runoff Muddies Waters for Would-be Liberal Leaders," *Globe and Mail*, 6 May 1989.

18 Campbell, "Eleven Men and a Constitution," 281.

19 Christopher Donville, "Join As an Equal Partner, Reform Party Tells Quebec," *Globe and Mail*, 30 Oct. 1989.

20 Keith Baldrey, "Reform Chief Hints at Entry in B.C. Vote," *Vancouver Sun*, 6 Dec. 1989.

21 Mulroney summed up the position sadly and correctly as the three-year period drew to a close. After noting his failure to anticipate the troubles threatening the accord, he continued: "I don't think that anybody fully understood the implications of the new constitutional provisions in 1982 that required [sic] a three-year wait before constitutional amendments could go through ... I thought, and many people thought, that within a matter of months after the signing on the third of June, 1987, that all the provinces would have ratified it ... Nobody anticipated that governments would change, signatures would be repudiated, and all of a sudden a very simple, straightforward document of unity would become a catch-all for everybody else's wish list as governments changed across the country." Susan Delacourt and Rhéal Séguin, "PM Scrambling to Save Meech Accord," *Globe and Mail*, 23 May 1990.

22 Lowell Murray, "The 1987 Constitutional Accord and Sexual Equality Rights," *CAUT Bulletin* (June 1988): 13.

23 See, however, the companion resolution announced by the first ministers after their final week-long closed bargaining session. This projected agenda for the future that failed to get unanimous agreement is best described as panic-determined. The *Vancouver Sun*, 12 June 1990, contains the final communiqué.

24 Campbell, "Eleven Men and a Constitution," 290.

25 *Report* (The Charest Report) of the Special Committee to Study the Proposed Companion Resolution to the Meech Lake Accord, *Minutes of Proceedings and Evidence of the Special Committee to study the Proposed Companion Resolution to the Meech Lake Accord*, 8–15 May 1990, no. 21.

26 Lysiane Gagnon, a generally moderate Quebec columnist for *La Presse*, reacted with fury to the Charest recommendations, which she

described as "this new grocery list, … this block of demands that they've hurled in our face to put us in our place." Graham Fraser, "PM Considers Bouchard's Offer to Resign," *Globe and Mail*, 22 May 1990. The same tone of anger and hurt pervades the resignation letter of Environment Minister Lucien Bouchard to Mulroney, in reaction to the Charest Committee's proposals. *Globe and Mail*, 23 May 1990 (Canadian Press translation).

27 J.A. Corry, "The Uses of a Constitution," in Law Society of Upper Canada, Special Lectures, *The Constitution and the Future of Canada* (Toronto 1978), 1–15.

28 Pierre Elliott Trudeau, *Federalism and the French Canadians* (Toronto 1968). For an incisive analysis of the personality and territorial principles and of federal language policy, see Kenneth McRoberts, "Making Canada Bilingual: Illusions and Delusions of Federal Language Policy," in David P. Shugarman and Reg Whitaker, eds., *Federalism and Political Community: Essays in Honour of Donald Smiley* (Peterborough 1989), 141–71.

29 For a helpful discussion, see Raymond Breton, "The Production and Allocation of Symbolic Resources: An Analysis of the Linguistic and Ethnocultural Fields in Canada," *Canadian Review of Sociology and Anthropology* 21 (May 1984): 123–44.

30 See O.P. Dwivedi et al, eds., *Canada 2000: Race Relations and Public Policy, Proceedings of the Conference held at Carleton University Ottawa, October 30–November 1, 1987* (Guelph 1989), for a valuable collection of articles on Canada's changing ethnic demography, visible minorities, and race relations.

31 William Thorsell, "Bilingualism No Longer the Language of Nationhood," *Globe and Mail*, 2 Sept. 1989.

32 For a clear statement of this position, see Manitoba Task Force on Meech Lake, *Report on the 1987 Constitutional Accord* (Winnipeg 1989), 12–16.

33 Laurence Grafstein, "*Look Back in Anger:* The 1987 Constitutional Accord, Report of the Special Joint Committee of the Senate and the House of Commons," *University of Toronto Faculty of Law Review* 46 (winter 1988): 227. A "substantial portion" of the briefs to the Manitoba Task Force expressed concern that the accord would weaken the Charter and persuaded the Task Force to recommend that the Charter be insulated from the section 2 interpretive clauses of the accord. Manitoba Task Force, *Report on 1987 Constitutional Accord*, 4, 25–7. In New Brunswick, "a major issue for presenters [to the Legislative Assembly Select Committee] was the need to define clearly and specifically the Charter's supremacy in the Constitution." Legislative Assembly of New Brunswick, Select Committee on the 1987 Constitutional Accord,

Final Report on the Constitution Amendment 1987 (Fredericton 1989),
42.

34 New Brunswick, Select Committee, *Final Report*, 44.

35 As the deadline approached, however, the groups speaking for official-
language minorities came to the support of the accord out of fear that
its defeat would encourage supporters of Quebec independence, which
might leave them worse off than they would be under Meech Lake.

36 Manitoba Task Force, *Report*, 69–71; New Brunswick, Select Committee, *Final Report*, 25–9. Although Newfoundland did not hold public
hearings, Premier Wells asserted that "perhaps the worst flaw in the
Accord was the closed process." "The Meech Lake Accord, An Address
to the Canadian Club of Montreal by Clyde Wells, 19 January 1990,"
mimeo, p. 1. Newfoundland's proposals to open up the process are
noted in "Constitutional Proposal 'An Alternative to the Meech Lake
Accord' Submitted by the Government of Newfoundland and Labrador
to the First Ministers' Conference November 9th and 10th, 1989," 7.

37 Attorney General for Ontario, "Brief to the Select Committee of the
Legislature on Constitutional Reform," mimeo, 4 May 1988, 79.

38 Ibid., 82.

39 Manitoba Task Force, *Report*, 5, 70.

40 "Globe and Mail–CBC News/Poll," *Globe and Mail*, 9 July 1990. In an
earlier poll, 58 per cent of Quebecers and 71 per cent of all Canadians
supported having a referendum on Meech Lake. Julian Beltrame,
"Canadians Want Meech Referendum, Poll Finds," *Globe and Mail*, 7
April 1990.

41 Charles Taylor, "Alternative Futures: Legitimacy, Identity and Alienation in Late Twentieth Century Canada," in Alan Cairns and Cynthia
Williams, eds., *Constitutionalism, Citizenship and Society in Canada*, Vol. 33
of the research studies of the Royal Commission on the Economic
Union and Development Prospects for Canada (Toronto 1985), 183–
229.

42 See also Trudeau's thesis that the contest between citizens and governments has been the big theme in recent Canadian constitutional history
and his related thesis linking the Charter to the sovereignty of the people. Donald Johnston, ed., *With a Bang, Not a Whimper, Pierre Trudeau
Speaks Out* (Toronto 1988), 46, 58, 94–5.

43 Jean Chrétien, "A Challenge of Leadership, A Speech Delivered ... to
the Faculty of Law, University of Ottawa, January 16, 1990," mimeo,
11; Daphne Bramham, "A 'Brooklyn Bridge' in Meech Proposal," *Vancouver Sun*, 7 June 1990 (re Blakeney).

44 Status Indians, of course, with their reserve land base are an exception.

45 For a discussion, see Peter H. Russell, "The Political Purposes of the
Canadian Charter of Rights and Freedoms," *Canadian Bar Review* 61

(1983): 30–54, and Alan C. Cairns, "The Canadian Constitutional Experiment," *Dalhousie Law Journal* 9 (Nov. 1984): 87–114.

46 See McRoberts, "Making Canada Bilingual," for a good discussion of the ideology of national integration that has provided the rationale for federal language policy since the "B & B" Commission, and its many weaknesses as a practical political theory.

47 Manitoba Task Force, *Report*, 25.

48 New Brunswick, Select Committee, *Final Report*, 42.

49 Clyde Wells, "Canadians Are Rejecting the Dismantling of Federalism," *Globe and Mail*, 14 April 1990.

50 *Globe and Mail*, 12 Feb. 1990. No breakdown was provided for differences in responses between French and English or Quebec and the rest of Canada.

51 Barbara Roberts, *Smooth Sailing or Storm Warnings? Canadian and Quebec Women's Groups on the Meech Lake Accord* (Toronto n.d.).

52 See *Un Dossier du Devoir: Le Québec et le Lac Meech* (Montreal 1987), 109–10, 123, 152–4, 157, 158–61, 180–1, 196, 252, 256; and Réal-A. Forest, dir., *L'adhésion du Québec à l'Accord du Lac Meech*, les Editions Thémis (Montreal 1988).

53 Andrée Lajoie et al, "Political Ideas in Quebec and the Evolution of Canadian Constitutional Law, 1945 to 1985," in Ivan Bernier and Andrée Lajoie, eds., *The Supreme Court of Canada as an Instrument of Political Change*, Vol. 47 of the research studies of the Royal Commission on the Economic Union and Development Prospects for Canada (Toronto 1986), 64. This view contrasts diametrically with the "purest liberalism" of Trudeau's views which lay behind the Charter, in which "only the individual is the possessor of rights." Individuals, according to Trudeau, are "not coercible by any ancestral tradition, being vassals neither to their race, nor to their religion, nor to their condition of birth, nor to their collective history." "The Values of a Just Society," in Thomas S. Axworthy and Pierre Elliott Trudeau, eds., *Towards a Just Society: The Trudeau Years* (Markham, Ont., 1990), 363–4.

54 William Thorsell, "Canadians Reclaim Their Many Solitudes," *Globe and Mail*, 23 Sept. 1989. An analysis of the Meech Lake debate in Quebec by Denis Robert confirms the accuracy of Thorsell's observation. "La signification de l'Accord du lac Meech au Canada anglais et au Québec francophone: un tour d'horizon du débat public," in Peter M. Leslie and Ronald L. Watts, eds., *Canada: The State of the Federation 1987–88* (Kingston 1988), 141–2, 149.

55 Cited in Calvin R. Massey, "The Locus of Sovereignty: Judicial Review, Legislative Supremacy, and Federalism in the Constitutional Traditions of Canada and the United States," *Duke Law Journal* 6 (1990): 1269.

56 Peter Hogg, "Federalism Fights the Charter of Rights," in Shugarman and Whitaker, eds., *Federalism and Political Community*, 252–3.

57 According to André Bzdera, representatives of Quebec's anglophone community "utilisent systématiquement une stratégie de 'lobbying judiciaire' visant à dérober l'Assemblée nationale de ses compétences au profit soit du gouvernement fédéral (anglophone), soit du pouvoir judiciaire canadien (anglophone)." "L'étude politique de la Cour suprême du Canada, le politologue québécois au banc des accusés," Communication pour présentation au colloque annuel de la Société québécoise de science politique, à l'Université Laval, 16 mai 1990, mimeo, 3.

58 F.L. Morton, Peter H. Russell, and Michael J. Withey, "The Supreme Court's First 100 Charter of Rights Decisions: A Quantitative Analysis," prepared for Annual Meeting, Canadian Political Science Association, 27–29 May 1991, Victoria, BC, 14–15.

59 Claude Morin, *Lendemains piégés: du référendum à la nuit des longs couteaux* (Montreal 1988), 282–3 (my translation).

60 The 1980 Beige Paper of the Constitutional Committee of the Quebec Liberal Party, *A New Canadian Federation* (Montreal 1980), had advocated a strong entrenched Charter with fewer concessions to the provinces – no notwithstanding clause, for example – than were in the actual Charter. Further, the proposals on mobility rights and minority-language rights did not contain the qualifications and exceptions of the 1982 Charter (31–3). Thus, on several key rights issues, at least in the immediate pre-referendum period, the Quebec Liberals were constitutionally closer to the federal Liberals than to the provincial PQ. In addition, Bourassa spoke favourably of the Charter prior to his 1985 election victory, and shortly after the election, Gil Rémillard, Quebec's minister for Canadian intergovernmental affairs, stated that Quebec would be willing to cede priority to the federal Charter over Quebec's Charter. (Campbell, "Eleven Men and a Constitution," 238, 239). On another occasion, Rémillard referred to the Charter as a "document of which we as Quebecers and Canadians can be proud ... We want Quebecers to have the same rights as other Canadians." ("Address by Mr. Gil Rémillard," in Peter M. Leslie, *Rebuilding the Relationship: Quebec and Its Confederation Partners: Report of a Conference Mont Gabriel, Quebec, 9–11 May, 1986* (Kingston 1987), 41.

61 Václav Havel, "History of a Public Enemy," *New York Review of Books*, 31 May 1990, 36.

Index

CPSIA information can be obtained at www.ICGtesting.com
Printed in the USA
LVOW130018071112

306150LV00002B/14/P